TRAVELLERS' TRAILS • IRELAND

TRAVELLERS' TRAILS • IRELAND

HUGH ORAM

PASSPORT BOOKS

NTC/Contemporary Publishing Group

This edition first published in 2001 by
Passport Books, an imprint of the
McGraw-Hill Companies

ISBN: 0-658-01543-5

Library of Congress Catalog Card Number: 2001131167

McGraw-Hill books are available at special quantity
discounts to use as premiums and sales promotions, or for
use in corporate training programs. For more information,
please write to the Director of Special Sales, Professional
Publishing, McGraw-Hill, Two Penn Plaza, New York,
NY 10121-2298. Or contact your local bookstore.

Contents

Glendalough, Co. Wicklow (see pp62–7)

Introduction

The aim of this guide book is to delve deeper than most other guides in order to get 'under the skin' of Ireland. Its range of varied and imaginative trails takes you across the length and breadth of the land, into the country's history and culture, exploring and revealing many facets of Irish life that have evolved over the centuries.

How to use this book

Divided into 24 trails of varying length, Travellers' Trails: Ireland enables you to explore Ireland, past and present. It follows themes of interest, and brings a special focus to individual communities and sites. It is not a hotel or restaurant guide, and should be used in conjunction with these. Use it by selecting the trail or trails you would like to follow. Each trail is conveniently sub-divided and given a length in part-days, days or weeks and you can "dip into" other trails in the area of the country you are in as you wish by consulting the index.

Whilst the longer trails are planned with the car driver in mind, it is worth noting that Ireland is good cycling country, and that often cycles may be hired in local centres for a more intimate exploration of the countryside than can be managed in a car. Routes have been described as clearly as possible, but as all drivers know, alterations and local diversions can sometimes be found. A good road atlas (minimum 4 miles to an inch) will be a useful help.

The Historical Background

The first settlers in Ireland were hunters, probably from Scotland, who arrived in Co Antrim c. 7000 BC. By 3000 BC tribes from the Mediterranean were building megalithic tombs all over Ireland which reveal a high degree of civilisation. The Celts arrived around 300 BC bringing their distinctive culture, laws and customs. In the fifth century St Patrick brought Christianity from Britain, establishing monasteries which became not only centres of learning but in effect small towns.

The monasteries drew scholars from all over Europe and, in turn, Irish missionaries took education and religion to every corner of Europe. At the same time craftsmen produced exquisite reliquaries, brooches, belts and personal adornments – this period is rightly known as the golden age.

The wealth of the monasteries and their towns attracted the Vikings, who settled around the coast. They were finally defeated by Brian Boru at the Battle of Clontarf in 1014 but on his death inter-kingdom rivalry led to chaos until the Normans arrived from England, bringing order and prosperity. They were so well assimilated into Irish society that the English crown decided a reconquest was needed. Ulster put up fierce resistance under Hugh O'Neill and Hugh O'Donnell but they were finally defeated at the Battle of Kinsale in 1601. Their exile and that of the Gaelic aristocracy is known as "The Flight of the Earls". The systematic dispossession of the natives and settlement of migrants from England and Scotland followed. The division of Protestant settler and native Catholic has had repercussions ever since.

Through the drastic exploits of Oliver Cromwell in Ireland to the defeat of James II by William of Orange at the Battle of the Boyne in 1690, to the harsh penal laws which followed the Treaty of Limerick, Ireland suffered many hardships, not least grinding poverty and recurrent food shortages. The Act of Union in 1800 abolished the Dublin parliament and removed power to London. Daniel O'Connell's election to Westminster (which, as a Catholic, he was forbidden to enter) led to the repeal of the more oppressive laws and to Catholic emancipation. A firm believer in non-violence, he came close to repeal of the union but his final years were clouded by the Great Famine when nearly a million died and two million emigrated.

Parnell became leader of the Home Rule Party in 1877, and with Gladstone's support, a Home Rule Bill nearly succeeded. Other leaders followed and in 1912 the Bill was passed. Ireland was to have self-government after World War I. Unionists in Ulster, however, armed themselves to fight to maintain the link with Britain. In Dublin, meanwhile, a group of volunteers decided they could not wait for the end of the war, and began the Easter Rising of 1916. Although unsuccessful and condemned by most Irish people, the execution of its leaders changed public opinion. The Anglo-Irish war lasted from 1919 to 1921.

The Treaty of 1921 gave independence to 26 of the 32 counties; six of the Ulster counties remained under British rule with a parliament at Stormont in Belfast. A section of the Republican movement opposed this compromise and a bitter civil war followed, culminating in the death of Michael Collins. World War II imposed great strains on the Free State (economically stagnant for many years) which stayed neutral. Sean Lemass later adopted a more vigorous, expansionist economic policy which brought new prosperity and paved the way for Ireland's entry into the EEC – now the EU – in 1972.

Today the Republic of Ireland is a parliamentary democracy with a president as head of state and two houses of parliament. Northern Ireland has suffered unrest since 1921, with the Civil Rights movement in 1968 calling for power sharing and equality in jobs and housing. Since then there has been extremist republican and loyalist paramilitary violence. A peace process, exemplified by a power-sharing executive at Stormont, has come about in recent years. Despite its somewhat beleaguered image, Northern Ireland is quite safe to visit.

TOURING AND TRANSPORT IN IRELAND

It is always worth contacting your local automobile association and the tourist board before touring. They will supply you with full details of the rules of the road, insurance, breakdown services, petrol, road signs, etc. You will need your driving licence and insurance certificate, and display a nationality plate if you are bringing your car into Ireland. The road network throughout Ireland is very extensive and while the principal highways are good those in more remote areas will vary. In the country watch out for sheep, cows and other animals being herded along the road.

Train services in the Republic are operated by Iarnrod Éireann–Irish Rail. Fast trains run from Dublin to the main population centres; the main train stations in Dublin are Connolly (Amiens Street) and Heuston (Kingsbridge). The

DART (Dublin Area Rapid Transit) is a marvellous way to get about on the 32km (20 mile) coastal line. Northern Ireland Railways (NIR) operate trains within Northern Ireland and run the Belfast–Dublin service jointly with Iarnrod Eireann; the main station in Belfast is Central Station.

Both Dublin and Belfast have extensive bus networks, run by Bus Átha Cliath/Dublin Bus and Translink/Citybus respectively. Ulsterbus run scheduled services out of town in Northern Ireland. The provincial bus network in Ireland is extensive; many private operators run services from Dublin to regional towns and cities. Many buses start from Busárus, the Central (Provincial) Bus Station in Store Street, Dublin. Public transport on Sundays is usually much reduced outside the cities and large towns.

Ireland also has a good air network, linking with other airports in Europe and internationally; the two largest airports are Dublin and Belfast International and both have full car-hire facilities.

LOCAL INFORMATION

Tourists and other visitors are strongly advised to check the opening times for buildings and sites before they set out. Quite often opening times can vary slightly from those given although, especially with country locations, a certain flexibility is shown. Whenever possible, the telephone numbers of individual tourist attractions are listed; during the peak summer period most larger towns in Ireland have Tourist Information Offices (TIOs) in operation with full access to information on local opening times. Local TIOs will also advise you on places to stay and tell you which accommodation is registered, a useful consumer safeguard.

GEOGRAPHY OF IRELAND

Ireland has an area of 84,421 sq km (32,595 sq miles). At its greatest points it is 486 km (302 miles) long and 275 km (171 miles) wide and consists of a central lowland surrounded by a broken range of hills and small mountains. There are thirty-two counties and four provinces: Connaught, Leinster,

Munster and Ulster. Six of the nine counties of Ulster are part of the United Kingdom and the other twenty-six form the Republic of Ireland. The population of the Republic is 3,500,000 and of Northern Ireland 1,580,000. Dublin is the capital of the former, with an urban population of about one million. The principal cities and towns are Dublin, Belfast, Cork, Derry, Limerick, Waterford and Galway. Of these only the first three have a population in excess of 100,000.

About 5 per cent of Irish land is under forest and coniferous trees grow particularly well in Irish soil. Over 350 forests are open to the public, and many are laid out with car parks, picnic areas, nature trails and walks. Ireland, as everyone knows, is very green. This is caused by the mild, damp climate which encourages lush growth. The Burren in Co Clare, however, is a lunar-like landscape of bare, carboniferous limestone.

There are at least 380 species of wild birds to be seen in Ireland, for migration goes on all year. The most common species are blackbird, thrush, goldcrest, starling and curlew. Among the indigenous animal species are the Irish hare, the Irish stoat, fox and red deer. Wild deer roam the Kerry and Wicklow mountains and are also to be seen in the Phoenix Park, Dublin. Irish horse breeding is world famous, being centred on counties Meath and Kildare. There are seven distinct breeds of Irish dog, the best known being the giant Irish wolfhound, the Irish setter and the Irish water spaniel. There is only one reptile, the common lizard, and, thanks to St Patrick – so the legend goes – no snakes!

WEATHER IN IRELAND

The Irish climate is mild on account of the Gulf Stream, without vast extremes of heat or cold. Average temperatures in January are 4–7º C and in July are14–16º C, although rising occasionally as high as 25º C. May and June are often the sunniest months, and North American visitors in particular will notice that there are many more daylight hours in summer than there. Rainfall is heaviest in the mountainous west and lightest in the east but the weather is at all times very changeable. A day of prolonged drizzle can end with a clear sky, a spectacular sunset and the promise of a sunny day to follow.

Even so, it is always wise to have a good raincoat or umbrella to hand while touring.

PUBLIC HOLIDAYS

In the Republic of Ireland the following are public holidays: 1 January, 17 March (St Patrick's Day), Easter Monday, first Monday in June, first Monday in August, last Monday in October, 25 December (Christmas Day) and 26 December (St Stephen's Day).

In Northern Ireland the holidays differ slightly: 1 January, 17 March (St Patrick's Day), Easter Monday, first and last Mondays in May, 12 July (Orangeman's Day), last Monday in August, 25 December (Christmas Day) and 26 December (Boxing Day).

TRAIL 1

Gaeltacht Areas

Some areas of west and south-west Ireland are designated Gaeltacht areas, where the Irish language is still a dominant language. In these areas, Irish culture is very much in evidence. Other smaller Gaeltacht areas exist, such as that in Ring, Co. Waterford and Rathcairn in Co. Meath. The Irish language has also been enjoying considerable revival in the North of Ireland, especially in west Belfast, where *Lá*, a daily newspaper in Irish, is published. In other parts of the country, the language is more diffuse.

DONEGAL

The Donegal Gaeltacht is one of the most extensive in the country, covering much of the western coast of the county and taking in Glencolumbkille, Dungloe and Dunlewy, up as far as Burtonport and Falcarragh, and including Arranmore Island and Tory Island. The Donegal Gaeltacht extends right up into north Donegal, to Downings and Fanad. For visitors to west Donegal, the main Irish language cultural college is run by Oídeas Gael in Glencolumbkille.

The Glencolumbkille Folk Village and Museum is steeped in Irish culture. The houses are exact replicas of those once occupied by inhabitants of this area. One of the houses dates from 1700, another from 1850 and a third from 1900; between them, they give a good idea of living conditions in the old times in west Donegal. Lots of household and farm artefacts are on view.

Oídeas Gael Centre, *Glencolumbkille, Co. Donegal; tel (073) 30248; fax (073) 30348; email oidsgael@iol.ie.*
Glencolumbkille Folk Village and Museum,
Glencolumbkille, Co. Donegal; tel (073) 30017 (open daily Easter–Oct).

Two islands in the Donegal Gaeltacht are well worth visiting, Tory Island and Arranmore Island.

Tory Island is 12 km (8 miles) from the mainland and is reached by ferry from Magheraroarty (there are also boats from Bunbeg). There are two services a day, all year round, but the weather is rough in winter. The island has one hotel with all facilities and its own school of primitive painting which was encouraged by the late Derek Hill, who often painted here. He died in 2000. The abundance of wildlife, including seabirds, is another attraction on Tory Island.

Arranmore Island is much easier to reach, since the boat trip only takes 20 minutes. Arranmore has spectacular cliffs, as well as sandy beaches, some attractive small villages and the only rainbow trout lake in Ireland. Daily sailings from Burtonport.

Tory Island ferry, *tel (075) 31991.*
Arranmore Island ferry, *tel (075) 20521.*

MAYO

In Co. Mayo, the Gaeltacht area is in the far west of the county, around Belmullet and including Achill Island. The traditional music school on Achill Island has been enjoying a great revival and has wonderful summer sessions.

GALWAY

The Galway Gaeltacht is the other big Irish-speaking area in the country, beginning at Furbo, just west of Galway city and extending through Spiddal and Inverin as far west as Recess. The Aran Islands too are an Irish language stronghold. Parts of the county east of Galway city are also designated Gaeltacht areas.

Padraig Pearse Cottage, Rosmuc, Co. Galway

One centre of interest is the Dan O'Hara Heritage Centre near Clifden, which incorporates the Connemara Heritage and History Centre. It gives a unique insight into the old ways of living.

The Padraig Pearse cottage near Rosmuc is well worth visiting – this was the summer home of the 1916 leader. The thatched cottage itself is very traditional, and the surrounding landscape of bogland and mountains is quite spectacular.

On the Aran Islands, the Aran Centre at Kilronan on Inishmore, the largest of the islands, will give a good insight into the island way of life, where Irish language and culture are still important. It also does daily screenings of the Man of Aran film, made on the island by Robert Flaherty in 1934. On Inishman, where Irish is still the everyday language, older women still wear the traditional colourful shawls and head-scarves, as well as calf-length woollen skirts. Innisheer, the smallest of the three islands, has a heritage house in the form of a traditional Aran Islands homestead, complete with thatched roof tied down against the wind. Inside, there are lots of details of everyday Aran life.

Dan O'Hara Heritage Centre, *Clifden, Co. Galway*; tel (095) 21246 (open daily March–Oct).

Padraig Pearse Cottage, *Rosmuc, Co. Galway; tel (091) 574292* (open daily mid June–mid Sept).

Aran Centre, *Inishmore, Aran Islands; tel (099) 61355* (open daily April–Oct).

Innisheer Heritage House, *Inisheer, Aran Islands; tel (099) 75021* (open daily April–Sept).

KERRY

The Co. Kerry Gaeltacht covers the Dingle pensinsula, including Dingle itself, as well as the area in south Kerry around Caherdaniel and Ballinskelligs.

The Blasket Island Centre at Ballinskelligs gives excellent insights into the culture, language and traditions of the Blasket Islands just offshore, and there are courses in Irish at An Diseart.

It's nearly 60 years since they were inhabited, but the Blaskets Islands had a tremendous tradition of Irish literature, producing such remarkable writers as Peg Sayers, Tomás Ó Criomhthain and Muiris Ó Súilleabháin.

Blasket Island Centre, *Ballinskelligs, Co. Kerry; tel (066) 9156444/9156371; fax (066) 9156446* (open daily April–Oct; Nov–March by arrangement).
Courses in Irish at: **An Diseart**, *The Celtic Education and Cultural Institute, Dingle, Co. Kerry; tel (066) 9152476.*

CORK

The Cork Gaeltacht areas are in the north-west of the county, around Ballyvourney and Ballingeary, known as Muskerry. The other stronghold of Irish is Cape Clear Island, a wonderful island off Baltimore in West Cork, which only has about 150 permanent inhabitants.

WATERFORD

The area around the fishing village of Ring in south Co. Waterford is a designated Gaeltacht area. Irish is still strong here, helped by the very active college. It's the smallest coastal Gaeltacht in Ireland, stretching from Ring to Old Parish, with just 800 inhabitants.

MEATH

The small area around Rathcairn, not far from Navan, is a Gaeltacht area, improbably near the capital. It's an artificially created Gaeltacht; the people were encouraged to settle here in the 1930s from western Ireland. The area around Gibbstown, just east of Kells, is also a designated Gaeltacht area and larger than that around Rathcairn. One of the most intriguing places to visit in this area is the Hill of Tara, with its deep insights into Celtic mythology.

DUBLIN

While Dublin may appear to be exclusively English speaking, the revival of Irish is proceeding at a pace, helped by thriving Gaelscoils, or Irish-speaking schools. Several organisations in the city organise Irish cultural events, including Gael Linn and Conradh na Gaeilge. Irish language radio programmes are broadcast by Raidió na Gaeltachta, while TG4 broadcasts TV

programmes mainly in Irish. For more information on Ireland's Gaeltacht regions, contact Gael Saoire.

Gael Linn, *26 Merrion Square, Dublin 2; tel (01) 676 7283.*
Conradh na Gaeilge, *6 Harcourt Street, Dublin 2; tel (01) 475 7401.*
Gael Saoire, *tel (066) 9152423; fax (066) 9152429; email info@gaelsaoire.ie; website www.gaelsaoire.ie.*

NORTHERN IRELAND

In the North too, enthusiasm for the Irish language is coming on fast. The 1991 census reported that over 140,000 people in the North were Irish speaking. One of the main annual events is Féile an Phobail, or the West Belfast festival, staged every August.

It stages a wide variety of community, social, entertainment and cultural events, with a strong emphasis on Irish as the spoken and written language; details from Féile an Phobail.

Another organisation in west Belfast that is very involved with Irish language and cultural events is An Cultúrlann McAdam-Ó Fiaich, named in honour of a Protestant Minister who was a devotee of the Irish language and the late Cardinal Ó Fiaich. The bookshop has the largest range of Irish language titles and teaching aids in the North of Ireland.

Féile an Phobail, Teach na Féile, *473 Falls Road, Belfast; tel (02890) 313440; fax (02890) 319150; email info@feileanphobail.ie; website www.info@feileanphobail.ie.*
An Cultúrlann McAdam-Ó Fiaich, *216 Falls Road, Belfast; tel (02890) 964180/964187; fax (02890) 964189.*

TRAIL 2

Canals

TWO WEEKS

During the space of two weeks, you should be able to sample most of Ireland's inland waterways, a truly rewarding experience. The three main inland waterways, the Grand Canal, the Royal Canal and the Shannon–Erne Waterway can be used by boat travellers. Other canal systems, especially the Newry Canal in the North and also the Ulster Canal, can only be experienced from the towpath. Another alternative is the River Barrow, not strictly speaking a canal, but whose navigation begins with a junction from the Grand Canal in Co. Kildare.

The best place to start a tour of Ireland's inland waterways is at the Waterways Centre at Ringsend in Dublin, just beside the start of the Grand Canal. This heritage centre will give you a good working knowledge of the history of Ireland's inland waterways, complete with fascinating three-dimensional layouts, maps, photographs, artefacts and an audio-visual presentation.

Further information on the inland waterways of Ireland can be obtained from Inland Waterways Ireland, a new all-Ireland body set up under the terms of the 1998 Belfast Agreement. The permanent headquarters will be in Enniskillen, with regional headquarters in Carrick-on-Shannon, Dublin and Scarriff, Co. Clare. In the period up to 2006, Waterways Ireland intends to oversee substantial further capital expenditure on the Grand Canal, the Royal Canal and the Barrow navigation.

Waterways Centre, *Ringsend, Dublin; tel (01) 677 7510* (open all year, daily).

Waterways Centre, Ringsend, Dublin

Inland Waterways Ireland, *17–19 Lower Hatch Street, Dublin 2; tel (01) 647 2535; fax (01) 678 7798.*

Grand Canal

The Grand Canal can be navigated over its entire 209 km (130 miles) length from Ringsend in Dublin, where it meets the Liffey, to the River Shannon at Shannonbridge, Co. Offaly. The canal goes through west Dublin suburbs; early sections, past Baggot Street bridge and Leeson Street, are interesting, but then it traverses the dreary industrial suburbs of west Dublin. Not until it reaches Co. Kildare does it resume a pleasant course. The canal will take you close to Edenderry and through Tullamore, before ending at the Shannon.

The Barrow Line offers an agreeable diversion. Turn off the Grand Canal in Co. Kildare. The first few miles of the Barrow are canalised, then you are into open river. The landscapes are quite spectacular, with distant views of the Wicklow mountains as you sail downstream. Villages along the way that make pleasant stopping off points include Leighlinbridge, Co. Carlow, while the first sizeable town is New Ross. Continue on to Waterford and its harbour, which will bring you to the sea.

Royal Canal

Again, a journey of several days. At present, the Royal Canal is not navigable for its entire length, including access to the River Liffey in Dublin, but substantial renovation work is under way and before long that shortcoming should have been remedied. Like the Grand Canal, the Royal Canal gets interesting once it leaves Dublin. The main town along its route is Mullingar. The other end of the Royal Canal, the last few miles to the Shannon, is being improved including the link to Longford town, and this should be open shortly.

Shannon–Erne Waterway

Once you reach the Shannon, sail north towards Carrick-on-Shannon, a wonderful stopping-off place. From Carrick, head north towards the Shannon–Erne waterway, which will bring you through such towns as Ballinamore and eventually into

Upper Lough Erne in Co. Fermanagh. You can make a diversion from the waterway into Lough Allen in Co. Leitrim, a marvellously unspoiled stretch of water. In Upper Lough Erne, you will see the entrance to the Ulster Canal, which is totally impassable. The Ulster Canal links Upper Lough Erne with Lough Neagh and has been closed for many years.

The original Ballinamore and Ballyconnell Canal had been opened in 1860 and closed in 1869, having been used by only eight boats. Work on its reconstruction began in 1991, cost over IR£30 million and was completed in 1994. Now the locks are electronically controlled. The canal itself is a joy to traverse, with such attractive villages along its route as Keshcarrigan and Ballinamore. Many tourist attractions have been developed along its route, so if you want to stop off along the way, there's plenty to do. One useful publication is the Shannon–Erne Users Guide by Dick Warner.

Survey work is under way to ascertain the feasibility of reconstructing the Ulster Canal, but if work does get under way, it's likely to take several years to complete. If the Ulster Canal is reopened, it would mean being able to navigate from the Shannon at Limerick through the entire length of Ireland, through the Lower River Bann to reach the sea by Coleraine.

On the Newry canal, just south of Portadown, you can visit Moneypenny's Lock. It's a restored lock keeper's house, together with stables and bothy, 3 km (2 miles) south of Portadown. It gives a useful insight into the old ways of canal working.

Also in the North, sections of the Newry Canal have been restored, including buildings, while the River Lagan presents a spectacular way into Belfast, culminating in the Lagan Lookout Centre. The centre explains the history of the weir on the river, as well as the river's history, using high-tech computer and video technology. The towpath beside the River Lagan can be walked from Lisburn to Stranmillis, a distance of 16 km (10 miles).

At the other end of the Shannon, much work is under way to reopen the Shannon to canal-type traffic from Limerick as far upstream as Killaloe. When this is completed, the Shannon will be entirely navigable as far as the Fermanagh lakes.

Shannon–Erne Waterway, *tel (078) 44855; fax (078) 44856; email shannonernepromo@eircom.net.*

Moneypenny's Lock, *near Portadown, Co. Armagh; tel (02838) 322205* (open weekends April–Sept).

Lagan Lookout Centre, *Donegall Quay, Belfast; tel (02890) 315444* (open daily April–Sept; Oct–March, Tues–Sun).

TRAIL 3

Tracing Your Ancestors

Tracing your ancestors is a fascinating task for countless visitors to Ireland each year. Some specific locations in central Dublin will go far towards helping your search along its way.

Begin with the National Library of Ireland in Kildare Street which has an office on the first floor dealing specifically with genealogical queries. It issues a number of leaflets on the subject, which will advise you on how to start, and its genealogy service is free.

Visitors can get expert advice on their research, together with access to reference material and help in finding aids. The redesigned website gives much greater access to the National Library's collections, including its database of newspapers. The genealogy service is of particular value to first-time researchers, but the Library also encourages more experienced family history researchers to continue using the facilities there.

The records in the National Library that are most used by family history researchers include parish records. The library has microfilm copies of almost all Roman Catholic parish registers up to about 1880. Most of the registers begin around 1810–1830, but in some counties, especially along the western seaboard, they begin later. On the other hand, some Leinster counties began their records in the 1780–1790 period and in cities, they started as early as 1760.

In the case of just three dioceses, Kerry, Limerick and Cashel, formal permission to consult registers has to be obtained from the diocese concerned. The National Library family history leaflet no. 2 has full details of how to do this.

National Library of Ireland, *Kildare Street, Dublin 2; tel (01) 603 0200; website www.nli.ie* (open all year, Mon–Fri l0am–5pm, Sat l0am–12.30pm).

Another superb source of information is the National Archives, which has census returns going back as far as 1821. There is the county by county Index of Surnames, recorded in *Griffith's Valuation* and the *Tithe Books*. This listing is invaluable in pinpointing relevant parishes and parish registers. The *Tithe*

Applotment Books were compiled between 1823 and 1837, and *Griffith's Valuation* was published between 1847 and 1864. Wills and will records are also stored here.

Trade and social directories are another source. The earliest provincial directories date from the 18th century; one of the first was *Ferrar's Directory of Limerick*, 1769. During the 19th century, countrywide directories were published, including *Pigot's Commercial Directory of Ireland* (1820 and 1824) and *Slater's Directories* (1846, 1856, 1870, 1881 and 1894). *Thom's Directory* contains an invaluable listing of streets, occupiers of houses and business. It has been published, annually, from the mid 19th century up to the present day. The full set of *Thom's Directories* can be consulted in the Dublin Corporation Archives.

National Archives, *Bishop Street, Dublin 8; tel (01) 407 2300; fax (01) 407 2333; email mail@nationalarchives.ie; website www.nationalarchives.ie* (open Mon–Fri, 9am–5.30 pm).

Dublin Corporation Archives, *Civic Museum, South William Street, Dublin 2; tel (01) 677 5877.*

Newspapers can be another valuable source of family information, for instance, notices of births, marriages and deaths. It is always helpful to have exact dates. *The Newsplan Directory* lists all the newspapers ever published in Ireland, while the National Library holds files of every issue published of the national newspapers in Ireland, as well as many local ones. National newspapers are held on microfilm, while many of the local newspapers are still in their easy-to-read original format.

The National Library's Department of Manuscripts holds the archives of many former landed estates throughout Ireland. These archives have records of the administration of these estates, including details of tenants. Other sources in the National Library include publications of local history societies, lists and records of trades and professions.

Details of births, marriages and deaths since 1864, and non-Roman Catholic marriages since 1845, are on record at the General Register Office. The Register of Deeds is also an invaluable source.

The Representative Church Body Library is a useful source of Church of Ireland records and the Presbyterian Historical Society has records relating to Presbyterians throughout Ireland. The Religious Society of Friends Library has detailed information on Quaker families throughout Ireland, while the Irish Jewish Museum has much material on Jewish families.

Also in Dublin, there's the Heraldic Museum which used to run a genealogical service, which was transferred to the National Library of Ireland next door. The Museum is the legal authority in Ireland on heraldry, granting and conferring arms. It also has displays of arms.

General Register Office, *8–11 Lombard Street East, Dublin 2; tel (01) 671 1000.*

Register of Deeds, *Henrietta Street, Dublin 1; tel (01) 670 7500.*

The Representative Church Body Library, *Braemor Park, Dublin 14; tel (01) 492 3979.*

Presbyterian Historical Society, *Church House, Fisherwick Place, Belfast; tel (02890) 323936.*

The Religious Society of Friends Library, *Swanbrook House, Morehampton Road, Donnybrook, Dublin 4; tel (01) 668 7157.*

Irish Jewish Museum, *3–4 Walworth Street, South Circular Road, Dublin 8; tel (01) 453 1797.*

Heraldic Museum, *Kildare Street, Dublin 2; tel (01) 603 0307.*

Throughout the country, another invaluable source of information on family history are the heritage centres in almost every county. As just one example, the Clare Heritage Centre, set in a converted Church of Ireland church, has extensive genealogical records on Clare people. During the 20 years immediately after the great mid l9th-century famine, it's estimated that 100,000 people at least left the county for foreign parts. The Clare Centre is an invaluable repository of genealogical material, as well as having many historical artefacts.

Clare Heritage Centre, *Corofin, Co. Clare; tel (065) 37955.*

In Northern Ireland, a good place to start is the Public Record Office of Northern Ireland – it's the major repository of genealogical source relating to Ulster. Visitors can do their own searches in the public search room. The General Register Office has records of births and deaths in Northern Ireland since 1864 and marriages since 1922.

A list is available, either from the National Library of Ireland in Dublin or the Public Records Office in Belfast showing all the genealogical research centres in the 32 counties of Ireland.

Public Record Office of Northern Ireland, *66 Balmoral Avenue, Belfast; tel (02890) 255905* (open Mon–Fri 9.15am–4.45pm, Thurs until 8.45pm).

General Register Office, *49 Chichester Street; tel (02890) 252000.*

TRAIL 4

Daniel O'Connell

Daniel O'Connell (1775–1847) was the great Irish politician who secured Catholic emancipation for Ireland and led the country along the road to constitutional reform that eventually resulted, in the early 20th century, in partial freedom for the southern part of Ireland. He was born near Cahirsiveen in Co. Kerry, was educated locally and then in Douai in France. He was called to the Bar in 1798. The rising in Ireland that year, and the violence that followed, confirmed O'Connell in his lifelong hatred of violence.

In 1823, O'Connell founded the Catholic Association to try and secure Catholic emancipation. In 1828, he was illegally elected MP for Co. Clare, with a huge majority of freeholders. Afraid of a widespread revolt, the British government conceded Catholic emancipation the following year, 1829. In 1830 he was the first Catholic to become an MP sitting at Westminster. The following year, he turned his attentions to the repeal of the 1801 Act of Union, which made Ireland and Britain into one kingdom. The parties at Westminster closed ranks against Daniel O'Connell, so he began organising monster repeal meetings in Ireland.

Daniel O'Connell's Coach, Derrynane

The largest gathering was at the historic Hill of Tara in Co. Meath, ancient seat of Ireland's kings. It attracted a crowd of one million. He planned the largest meeting of all for Clontarf, Dublin, but the authorities banned it and rather than risk a violent confrontation, O'Connell called it off. In 1844, he spent four months in a Dublin prison, which had a seriously adverse affect on his health. From that year onward,the differences grew between O'Connell and the increasingly revolutionary Young Ireland movement.

The repeal movement faded and the great famine, which started in 1845 and lasted until 1849, devastated Ireland; O'Connell's dreams of peaceful constitutional reform were dashed. In January 1847, he made a last desperate plea in the House of Commons for help for the famine victims in Ireland. The following month, he left for Rome, but becoming more seriously ill, he never got further than Genoa, where he died on 15 May 1847.

SOUTH KERRY

ONE DAY

Two locations in south Co. Kerry can be seen within the space of one day: they give dramatic testimony to O'Connell's life story. He was born just outside Cahirsiveen, but there is little left to see today except the ivy-covered ruins of Carhan House, which stands beside the river of the same name.

In Cahirsiveen itself, the O'Connell Memorial Church was opened in 1888; it was built with Newry granite and dressed with locally quarried black limestone. The tower of the church was never completed. The nearby heritage centre, in the old RIC barracks that look like a Walt Disney fort, has much material on the life and times of Daniel O'Connell. The barracks were built in 1875 as a replacement for earlier and smaller buildings, and were burned out by Republican forces in August 1922. The ruins lay dormant until 1992, when restoration began to turn the old buildings into a heritage centre.
Cahirsiveen Heritage Centre, *Cahirsiveen, Co. Kerry; tel (066) 94727777* (open daily throughout the year).

From Cahirsiveen, travel 32 km (20 miles) along the N70, otherwise known as the Ring of Kerry. It's a spectacularly beautiful road, with views of mountains and sea; you will pass through just one small town en route, Waterville.

At Caherdaniel, take the turn for Derrynane, the great house and estate that belonged to O'Connell and which is now in State care. The estate covers a total of 130 hectares (320 acres). The house itself was built by O'Connell in 1825 and the east and south wings have been untouched since then. The dining room and the drawing room are furnished in the style of that period – all the furniture was made by Irish craftspeople, including tables and chairs. The ground-floor dining room also has many family portraits.

The drawing room on the first floor has as its centrepiece the magnificent table presented to O'Connell when he was an alderman in Dublin Corporation. The base of the table is made from Irish oak and features carvings of Irish wolfhounds and a harp. The top is made of walnut. The great chair in this room was often used by O'Connell. You can also see the chapel, which O'Connell had built in 1844 to commemorate his release from prison. In a small room, just off the ground-floor entrance, you can see many of his mementoes, including correspondence from his last journey as far as Genoa.

The great spaces of Derrynane National Historic Park are well worth exploring. The estate contains many nature trails, through woodlands and flower gardens, past the bird sanctuary, while there's an extensive stretch of coastline with a sandy beach. At low tide, you can walk across to Abbey Island and explore the remains of Derrynane Abbey.

Derrynane, *near Caherdaniel, Co. Kerry; tel (066) 9475113* (open May–Sept, Mon–Sat 9am–6pm, Sun 11am–7pm; April and Oct, Tues–Sun 1pm–6pm; Nov–March, Sat–Sun 1pm–6pm).

DUBLIN AND CO. MEATH

ONE DAY

In Dublin, you can see the exterior of Number 58 Merrion Square, which O'Connell bought in 1814. O'Connell did much of his work here, starting at 5am every morning. At 10.30am every weekday morning, he walked to the Four Courts, came home for dinner at 4pm and worked until

O'Connell's House, Derrynane, Co. Kerry

bedtime. Also in Dublin, you can see his statue that stands on O'Connell Street, near O'Connell Bridge. Some of the figures on the statue still have bullet holes from the 1916 Rising.

HILL OF TARA

ONE DAY

The Hill of Tara is 38 km (24 miles) north of Dublin on the N3, turn off indicated just before Navan. The great hill has many historic connotations, dating back to pre-Christian Celtic times. It was the seat of the High Kings of Ireland until it was abandoned in 1022. The present-day hill is full of history, a peaceful oasis that is also a good lookout point in clear weather over much of central Ireland. Just before he was imprisoned in 1844, O'Connell came here for the largest of his repeal meetings; one million people came to listen.

Aerial view of the Hill of Tara, Co. Meath

TRAIL 5

The 1798 Rising

The 1798 Rising, which began in Co. Wexford, was a deeply symbolic rebellion against British administration in Ireland and was the first in a series of uprisings that culminated in the 1916 Easter Rising. It began simply enough, with the burning of the Catholic chapel in the village of Boolavogue, 8 km (5 miles) south-east of Ferns, Co. Wexford. The curate at Boolavogue, Fr Murphy, led a group of local insurgents who took up arms and pikes against the Crown forces. From that single incident developed a whole series of skirmishes that only ended at the final battle of 1798, at Vinegar Hill in Enniscorthy. For some months, it looked as if the rebellion could pose a serious challenge to the authority of Dublin Castle and although it was eventually put down, with much brutality, it sowed further seeds of rebellion that were to manifest themselves throughout the 19th century, for instance in 1803, 1848 and 1867.

WEXFORD

ONE DAY

This tour of Enniscorthy and district begins at the Fr Murphy Centre in Boolavogue. The rural cottage where Fr Murphy lived has been restored to its original state; the gable wall of the restored cottage is the original wall of his house. Other buildings that have been restored on the farmstead include the pigsty, the cow-house, the barn and the stable. Around the farmyard, stones have been engraved with the names of people who died in the uprising.

Fr Murphy Centre, *Boolavogue, Co. Wexford; tel (054) 66898* (open Easter–Oct, Mon–Sat l0am–5.30pm, Sun 11am–7pm; Nov, Sun lpm–4pm; Dec–Feb, by appointment only).

From Boolavogue, return to the main N11 and continue for 13 km (8 miles) south-east to Enniscorthy, which has several sites relevant to 1798.

The National 1798 Visitor Centre was opened in 1998 to commemorate the 200th anniversary of the rising. It has a very impressive electronic presentation, with images, graphics and sound, concluding with a multimedia re-creation of the Battle of Vinegar Hill. The centre also has a number of artefacts from the period, such as pikes, that visitors can handle for themselves and it puts the 1798 Rising in both its national and international context.

When you leave the bridge over the River Slaney in Enniscorthy town centre, turn left into Mill Park Road and continue for 500 metres. The centre is well signposted.

National 1798 Visitor Centre, *Enniscorthy, Co. Wexford; tel (054) 37596/7; fax (054) 37198; email 98com@iol.ie; website www.wexford.ie* (open all year, Mon–Sat 9.30am–6pm, Sun 11am–6pm).

Return to the town centre and the County Museum, unmistakably set in the old castle. The castle dates back to 1205 and over the years it has had a variety of uses – in the late 19th century, it even became the offices of a local newspaper. It was used as a residence until 1951 and converted into the county museum in 1961. The museum has four main sections on several floors depicting the history of Co. Wexford through the centuries.

Military history features strongly and in the 1798 section, there's a collection of pikes. True to its rebellious nature, Enniscorthy was one of the few places outside Dublin to actively support the 1916 Easter Rising in Dublin and the 1916 section has many photographs and other artefacts depicting the town's participation.

Enniscorthy County Museum, *Enniscorthy, Co. Wexford; tel (054) 35926; email wexmus@iol.ie* (open June–Sept, Mon–Sat 10am–1pm, 2pm–6pm, Sun 2pm–5.30pm; Oct–Nov 2pm–5.30pm daily; Dec–Jan, Sun 2pm–5pm; Feb–May, 2pm–5.30pm daily).

Also in the centre of Enniscorthy, you can see the memorial to 1798 in Market Square. It depicts Fr Murphy, the leader of the rising, and a pikeman. The memorial was the work of Oliver Sheppard, who created the statue of Cúchulainn in the GPO, Dublin. In Abbey Square, the memorial portrays Seamus Rafter, a local leader of the 1916 Easter Rising.

From most parts of Enniscorthy, you cannot help but see Vinegar Hill. It's not high – 118 metres (390 ft) – but it's an outstanding viewpoint. From the top, you can see over Enniscorthy town, including Pugin's great cathedral, as far as the Blackstairs mountains in the west and the Wicklow mountains in the north.

Vinegar Hill was the site of the last battle of 1798, when 14,000 rebels, mostly armed with pikes and pitchforks, and only a few hundred with firearms, faced the might of Crown forces led by Johnson and Lake. The 1798 rebels held the hill from 28 May 1798, when they captured Enniscorthy, forcing the British garrison to withdraw to Wexford, until their last stand on 21 June. Preserved on the hilltop, as a national monument, is the stump of an old windmill. An old iron door, shattered by cannonfire, is preserved inside.

From Enniscorthy, drive the 20 km (12 miles) south along the N11 to Wexford town. The rebels were very active here too, and for a month in 1798 held the town against Crown forces. The 1798 memorial in the Bull Ring, by Oliver Sheppard, commemorates the men of Wexford in 1798.

From Wexford, you can return to Dublin, where further events of 1798 are depicted. Return along the main N11, taking a diversion into Arklow town. There, a statue of Fr Murphy can be seen standing outside the Catholic church in Main Street. From Arklow, take the R747 through Tinahely to Baltinglass. In Baltinglass, take the N81 in the Dublin direction as far as Donard. The drive from Arklow to Donard is about 40 km (25 miles) but it traverses the rewarding landscapes of south Co. Wicklow.

Signposted from Donard – it's a distance of 9 km (4 miles) south-east of the village – is the Dwyer–McAllister cottage. This building is well worth seeing; the cottage has been restored to its original state, as it was when used by rebel leaders Dwyer and McAllister in 1798, and it gives a fine sense of the rural isolation of those times.

Dwyer–McAllister Cottage, *near Donard, Co. Wicklow* (open daily, June–Sept, 2pm–6pm).

Also take a detour to Carlow. On 25 May 1798, 640 United Irishmen were killed in a battle with Crown forces in Tullow

Dwyer-McAllister Cottage, Donard, Co. Wicklow

Street, Carlow. About 400 of them were buried in gravel pits on the Graiguecullen side of the town; they are commemorated by a Celtic monument at Governey Park.

DUBLIN

ONE DAY

Further 1798 locations can be visited in Dublin. The Liberties was the main centre, since many of the residents gave shelter to insurgents on the run from the rising in counties Wexford, Wicklow and Kildare. Many pikes were secreted in the area. One of the supporters of the rising in Dublin, Lord Edward Fitzgerald, was captured in the area on 19 May 1798 and died in prison shortly afterwards.

The area of Smithfield just across the river was a designated assembly point for the insurgents in 1798. Dublin Castle noted that after sunrise the lanes and alleyways to Smithfield were found to be full of pikes and muskets which the rebels had dropped in their retreat. Just in front of the former barracks that now house the National Museum of Ireland extension can be seen a large football pitch, known as Croppies Acre. This in fact was the burial ground where hundreds of supporters of the 1798 Rising were buried after being captured and tortured in May of that year. The barracks themselves held Theodore Wolfe Tone, father of Irish Republicanism, after his capture in Letterkenny, Co. Donegal. Wolfe Tone subsequently died in prison in November 1798.

TRAIL 6

Architecture, Old and New

Throughout Ireland, especially in urban areas, many excellent examples of 18th- and 19th-century architecture (and sometimes earlier) survive, alongside more modern work carried out during the 20th century. Several regions are outstanding for their architecture: Dublin, Kilkenny, Cork, the Midlands, the North and the West.

DUBLIN

ONE DAY

A day's concentrated sightseeing should embrace a good cross-section of old and new architecture.

Begin at Dublin Airport. The modern terminal, opened in 1972 and expanded over the intervening years, is largely devoid of any architectural merit – it's purely functional, with little nod in the direction of aesthetics – but the original terminal building, opened in 1940, is entirely different. It was designed by Desmond FitzGerald, brother of Dr Garret FitzGerald, a former Taoiseach. Even though the building is

The Custom House, Dublin

now totally overshadowed by more modern buildings surrounding it, you can still see its elegant art deco lines from near the modern terminal building. It's best seen from the outside; the interior has been so altered that little remains of its original layout. The old terminal recalls the distant and long gone days of aviation, when flying was graceful and elegant and passengers dressed almost as if they were going to the races.

In Dublin city centre, if you travel by bus from Dublin Airport, you will be deposited at Busárus in Store Street. Again, a modern building that has stood the test of time. Designed by Michael Scott, it was opened in 1948 as a combination of Government offices and bus terminus. For such a utilitarian mixture of uses, the building is light and airy in its main concourse, with a striking exterior. It has weathered surprisingly well.

From Busárus, cross the road to the Custom House, designed by Gandon in the late 18th century. It was built on land reclaimed from the River Liffey and opened in 1792. During the War of Independence (1919–1921) it was set on fire and badly damaged. Much of the subsequent restoration work was poorly executed, but during the 1980s lengthy restoration work on the external and internal fabric righted those wrongs and brought the whole building, including its external statues denoting the rivers of Ireland, back to their pristine state. The Custom House also has a visitor centre that depicts the history of the building and its reconstruction. The **Custom House**, *Dublin; tel (01) 679 3377* (open Mon–Fri, all year).

From Busárus, walk 500 metres up Talbot Street and into Marlborough Street. The pro-Cathedral is one of the most elegant city centre buildings, built in the early 19th century and remarkably similar in its architectural style to the church of St Philippe du Roule in Paris. With its elegant Corinthian columns and lofty interiors, the building is a fine example of early 19th-century ecclesiastical architecture.

The General Post Office in O'Connell Street dates from the same period and was designed by Francis Johnston in 1814. It was largely destroyed during the 1916 Easter Rising, but was reconstructed during the 1920s.

From the GPO, walk along the north quays of the

River Liffey. Along the way, at Ormond Quay, you will see an outstanding example of contemporary architecture at Morrisons Hotel, opened in 1999. Continue further along the quays, to the Four Courts, similar in date and style to the Custom House and likewise damaged during the troubles in earlier 20th-century Ireland. The building was badly damaged by fire in 1922, but subsequently restored. You can inspect the interior, under the great cupola, and climb to the viewing gallery on the roof.

At the back of the Four Courts is Smithfield, once a great square surrounded by distilleries. The distilleries are long gone, although their historical heritage is well recalled in the Old Jameson Centre. In and around the square, considerable construction work has brought a new sense of life. The old distillery chimney has been restored as a viewing platform and is the best alternative to Nelson's Pillar, outside the GPO, blown up in 1966.

Cross the river to the new Dublin Corporation offices at Wood Quay. Designed by Sam Stephenson, the first block caused howls of outrage, particularly because of its brutalist design and because the site was once the centre of Viking Dublin. The second and more modern block, facing the river, is less austere and more forgiving, with bright, airy spaces inside that are often used for exhibitions. Designed by Scott Tallon Walker, its frontage adds to the river landscape, while the most striking interior feature is the atrium, complete with internal garden.

Dublin Corporation Offices, *Wood Quay, Dublin;* (open all year, Mon–Fri).

Behind the Civic Offices are Christchurch Cathedral and then St Patrick's Cathedral. The former dates to the 12th century, while the latter is largely a 19th-century reconstruction. From St Patrick's Cathedral, walk the short distance to Parliament Street and the start of Temple Bar.

The whole Temple Bar district, from here to Westmoreland Street, has been revived. Many 18th-century brick buildings have been revitalised, while many modern ones have been blended in. The Irish Film Centre in Eustace Street is one good example of merging old and new; it used to be the old 19th-century Quaker Meeting House, and now houses two

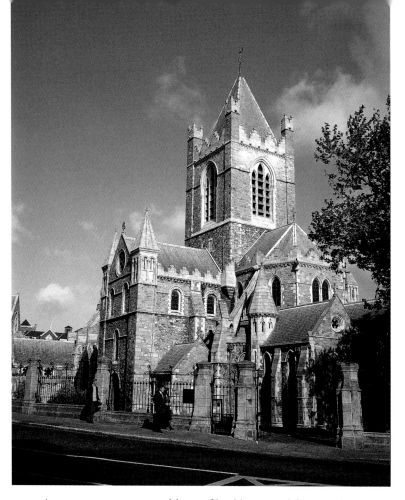

Christchurch Cathedral, Dublin

cinemas, a restaurant and bar, a film library and film archives. Meeting House Square, just at the side of the Irish Film Centre, is a great gathering place. Other buildings worth seeing include the Green Building, which contains eight apartments and is designed to be 80 per cent energy self-sufficient.

The Temple Bar Gallery and Printworks is at a corner of Temple Bar Square, the other great meeting area in the district. The gallery is designed in prismatic form, taking inspiration from early Cubist paintings and it contains 30 artists' studios. The Arthouse multimedia centre for the arts and the Ark children's cultural centre are also worth an inspection. All in all, Temple Bar provides a useful mingling of 18th- and 19th-century shop and workshop buildings and houses, and late 20th-century architecture, creating a district within an urban area that's unique in Ireland.

Dublin Castle, including the Chester Beatty Library, is on the opposite side of Dame Street from Temple Bar. The castle was built in the 13th century and until 1922 was the seat of British administration in Ireland. It's a vast sprawling complex, with some unimpressive modern additions. However, the State Apartments are worth seeing, including St Patrick's Hall, the main one. The Church of the Most Holy Redeemer, in the lower castle yard, was designed in the first decade of the 19th century by Francis Johnston. He was the architect of the GPO in O'Connell Street.

The Chester Beatty Library opened at Dublin Castle in 2000, having transferred from Shrewsbury Road, Ballsbridge. The new library consists mainly of the renovated Clock Tower building, with a modern addition for the entrance area. The library contains one of the finest collections of Islamic and Asian art in the world.

Chester Beatty Library, *Dublin Castle, Dublin; tel (01) 407 0750* (open daily, all year).

At the Trinity College end of Temple Bar is one of the great buildings of 18th-century Dublin, the Bank of Ireland. Originally built as the Houses of Parliament for Ireland, a role it served until the Act of Union (1801), the interior has been

carefully preserved, even though it's a working bank, and can be visited daily, Mon–Fri.

Walk from the Bank of Ireland along Nassau Street into South Leinster Street and Merrion Square, about 1 km (0.8 mile). Merrion Square was one of the two great squares built in Dublin in the 18th century. The brick facades remain as they were – at Number 29, on the corner of Lower Fitzwilliam Street and Upper Mount Street, you can visit an exact reconstruction of a late 18th-century house with everything perfect, down to the small-

Georgian doorway, Merrion Square, Dublin

39

est items of furniture and the wallpaper. Sadly, the rest of the Georgian terrace in Lower Fitzwilliam Street was torn down by the ESB in the 1960s to make a headquarters of hideous design and proportions. Ironically, the ESB is preparing to move its corporate headquarters elsewhere, leaving this lamentable design behind.

Number 29 Merrion Square, *Dublin; tel (01) 702 6165* (open daily, all year, for tours).

The nearby Fitzwilliam Square is smaller and more enclosed than Merrion Square, but is equally perfectly preserved. The gardens in the centre of Fitzwilliam Square are not open to the public; those in Merrion Square are.

You may also wish to visit the Irish Architectural Archives, which contain much material on Ireland's architectural history.

Irish Architectural Archives, *44/45 Merrion Square, Dublin; tel (01) 676 3430; fax (01) 661 6309; email iaal@iaa.iol.ie* (open all year, Tues–Fri).

The tour concludes at Sandymount on Dublin Bay, where the old Martello Tower, built in the early years of the 19th century, has been desecrated by shutters put up for a restaurant that functioned here briefly. However, the main structure of the tower is intact. A number of these Martello towers can be seen along the east coast, including Portmarnock, Howth, Dalkey Island and Bray.

MIDLANDS

TWO DAYS

A number of locations scattered throughout the Midlands will make an interesting tour spread over two days, beginning on the east coast in Drogheda.

Drogheda, although much developed in recent years, still has much of interest, including its quayside warehouses, dating from the 18th and 19th century. The railway viaduct, built in the mid 19th century, is perhaps the greatest feat of early railway architecture and engineering in Ireland. In the town itself, St Peter's Catholic Church in West Street is complemented by St Peter's Church (formerly Church of Ireland) at the top of Peter Street. The Drogheda Heritage Centre has many artefacts relating to the town.

Just outside the town centre, on the Dublin side of the river, the old military barracks, dating from the early 19th century, have been converted into Millmount Museum and various craft workshops. The nearby tower, which gives the best view over the town, has been restored and there are plans to place historic exhibits inside.

Drogheda Heritage Centre, *Mary Street, Drogheda, Co. Louth; tel (041) 9836643* (open Oct–May, Mon–Fri 10am–5pm, Sun 2pm–6pm; June–Sept, also Sat 10am–5pm). **Millmount Museum**, *Drogheda, Co. Louth; tel (041) 9833097* (open all year, Mon–Sat 9am–5pm, Sun 2pm–5pm).

From Drogheda, travel to Newgrange in the Boyne Valley, 8 km (5 miles). The ancient tumulus at Newgrange is the most spectacular example of early Irish architecture, built all of 5,000 years ago. It's a very popular site, so to relieve the pressure of visitor numbers, the Brú na Bóinne Heritage Centre was built nearby. It's very modern, very functional and very appropriate for the landscape, and gives a good insight into this prehistoric site.

Brú na Bóinne Heritage Centre, *Newgrange, Co. Meath; tel (041) 9880300* (open daily, March–April 9.30am–5.30pm; May 9am–6.30pm; June–mid Sept 9am–7pm; mid Sept–end Sept 9.30am–6.30pm; Oct 9.30am–5.30pm; Nov–Feb 9.30am–5pm).

From Newgrange, it's a 50 km (31 miles) drive south, into Co. Kildare. The Kildare Hotel and Country Club at Straffan, not far from Maynooth, is a fine conversion of an 18th-century great mansion. The main part of the hotel is a sensitive conversion and if you repair there for drinks or a meal, you can inspect the architectural delights as well as one of the largest privately held collections of Jack B. Yeats (1871–1957), brother of W.B. Yeats. In his lifetime his paintings, especially his large-scale oils, were seen as very avant-garde. Today he's regarded as one of the most important Irish artists.

From Straffan, return to the main road west, the N4, and continue to Mullingar (50 km/31 miles), where the

Kilkenny Castle, Kilkenny

Cathedral of Christ the King is a remarkable piece of 20th-century architecture, dedicated in 1939. Two of its chapels are adorned with mosaics created by a Russian artist, Boris Anrep.

There's a plan to built a national transport museum in Mullingar, with many of the railway buildings restored to their late 19th-century state, but this is unlikely to be ready until at least 2002.

Near Mullingar (5 km/3 miles south) is the newly restored Belvedere House and gardens, brought back to their 18th-century magnificence. The house was probably designed by Richard Cassels, who also designed Russborough House, near Blessington, Co. Wicklow. The gardens include three terraces looking out over Lough Ennell.

Belvedere House and Gardens, *near Mullingar, Co. Westmeath; tel (044) 49060* (open daily, April–Aug 10.30am–7pm; Sept–Oct 10.30am–6.30pm; Nov–March 10.30am–4pm).

From Mullingar, travel 100 km (62 miles) south to Kilkenny, Ireland's medieval city.

Here, the outstanding buildings include Rothe House in the High Street, which was built in 1594 as a merchant's house and which is now a museum, and the Tholsel, the town hall, dating back to a restoration in 1761. Smithwicks brewery was founded in 1710 and the grounds include a ruined abbey.

Kilkenny Castle was built between 1192 and 1207 and was the main seat of the Butler family from the 14th century until 1967, when it was given to the people of Kilkenny. It has been extensively restored; outstanding features include the Long Gallery. St Canice's Church of Ireland cathedral was built in the 13th century and is the second longest in Ireland. Finally, a more modern building is the Kilkenny Design Centre, which was set up in the castle stables in the 1960s.

Smithwicks Brewery, *Kilkenny; tel (056) 21014* (tours all year, Mon–Fri).

Kilkenny Castle, *Kilkenny; tel (056) 21450* (open daily, April–May 10.30am–5pm; June–Sept 10am–7pm; Oct–March, Tues–Sat 10.30am–12.45pm, 2pm–5pm, Sun 11am–12.45pm, 2pm–5pm).

LIMERICK AND GALWAY

TWO DAYS

Limerick has a fine if somewhat neglected reputation for good architecture. At the very start of the city centre, the new location for the Hunt Museum represents a reworking of the 18th-century Custom House. Nearby, St Mary's Church of Ireland Cathedral has many old relics; it dates from the 12th century.

Also in Limerick, see the Georgian splendour of Pery Square, the finest Georgian architecture in Ireland outside Dublin. Number 2 has been preserved in its pristine state. About 15 km (10 miles) from Limerick is the village of Adare. With its Main Street lined with thatched cottages, it is arguably the most picturesque village in Ireland.

GALWAY

ONE DAY

For such a large, thriving city, the capital of Connemara is surprisingly deficient in good architecture. The Catholic cathedral is worth seeing, if only for its awfulness. It's a modern building, built in the late 1950s from black Galway "marble", which is in fact limestone – the cathedral is singularly lacking in either taste or subtlety. More reverence can be accorded St Nicholas Church in the city centre, which was begun about 1320 and enlarged in the 15th and 16th centuries.

From Galway, take the 100 km (62 mile) drive west to Kylemore Abbey in Connemara. Although it's now a tourist trap, the abbey itself, built in the 1860s, has been largely untouched and the miniature Gothic church (1868) in its grounds is a small-scale replica of Norwich Cathedral.

Kylemore Abbey, *Kylemore, Co. Galway; tel (095) 41146; website www.kylemoreabbey.com* (open all year daily, 9am–5.30pm, closed Christmas week and Good Fri. Gardens open daily Easter–Sept, 10.30am–4.30pm).

CORK AND TIPPERARY

TWO DAYS

Parts of Co. Cork deserve close architectural inspection. Start your journey of discovery in the marvellous seaside town of Youghal, east Cork. Although much development has taken place in the past few years, the basics of Youghal are untouched, including the late 18th-century Clock Tower, medieval houses along the Main Street and the town walls, which are surpassed in scale in Ireland only by those in Derry. They were built in the 13th century and extended in the 17th century. Among the really outstanding domestic dwellings are the Red House, a good example of early 18th-century Dutch architecture and the Elizabethan almhouses, built in 1610.

From Youghal, travel 60 km (37 miles) north-west to the market town of Mitchelstown to see the Georgian buildings in Kingston College, which is actually a square. The square was built in 1775 and although it has been badly neglected in recent years, a refurbishment programme that will honour its original architectural integrity is underway.

From Mitchelstown, travel 40 km (24 miles) east to Clonmel, with its West Gate (originally 14th century, restored 1831) and the Main Guard, built in the late 17th century. Also worth seeing in Clonmel are the quaysides, with old warehouses and houses and the brand-new Tipperary County Museum, the first county museum built in the history of the State. The collection has been extended to include many facets of life in the county.

Tipperary County Museum, *Emmet Street, Clonmel, Co. Tipperary; tel (052) 25399; fax (052) 80390; email pholland@southtipp.coco.ie* (open daily, all year).

Clonmel to Cashel is 20 km (12 miles) along the R688. The Rock of Cashel has the most magnificent set of medieval ecclesiastical buildings in Ireland, including ruins of a cathedral, Cormac's Chapel and a round tower. It's open daily, all year. The Church of Ireland cathedral dates from the 18th century, while in the 1836 Bolton Library there is a very extensive collection of medieval and other rare books.

Return to Cork city, 96 km (60 miles). Parts of the city are grimy, but it has many fascinating architectural delights. A late Victorian bank in the city centre has been converted into headquarters for the Irish Examiner newspaper group, surely the most sumptuous newspaper headquarters in Ireland. Also in Cork, see St Anne's Church (1722) in Shandon, with the famous bells. St Finbarr's Cathedral (Church of Ireland) was built in the 1860s in an exuberant French Gothic style. On the other hand, Turner's Cross Church (1937) on the northside heights is modern and minimalistic. From the city, it's a striking addition to the skyline, while from the front of the church, virtually the whole of Cork city can be seen. Modern buildings of note in Cork include the Opera House and the Gate Multiplex, the latter opened in 1999.

Drive 35 km (20 miles) south-east of Cork to Kinsale, a small seaside town with several architectural gems. St Multose Church dates mainly to the 14th century. Although now overshadowed by the new hostel built insensitively alongside the church, St Multose is still worth seeing for its interior. Another church worth seeing in Kinsale is the Carmelite church. The old French prison dates back to the 15th century; this square tower has now been converted to a wine museum. Also in Kinsale, see the old town corporation offices, converted into the town museum. Close to Kinsale, Charles Fort and James Fort, both 17th century, are still impressive fortifications.

One final port of call is Clonakilty, 40 km (24 miles) west of Kinsale. One of the architectural gems of Clonakilty is Emmet Square, Georgian in its style. The model town in Clonakilty features all the main towns in West Cork, in miniature, with the bright colours of many houses faithfully reproduced.

Clonakilty Model Town, *Clonakilty, Co. Cork; tel (023) 33224* (open daily, July–Aug 10am–6pm; Feb–June, Sept–Oct 11am–5pm).

BELFAST

ONE DAY

See the City Hall, the Grand Opera House and the brand-new Odyssey Centre, one of the most striking of many modern buildings in Belfast. The City Hall was built in 1906 and it is a magnificent if slightly over-the-top edifice in Portland stone. **Belfast City Hall**, *Belfast; tel. (02890) 270456* (guided tours Mon–Fri, all year).

Almost opposite the City Hall is the late 18th-century Linenhall Library. The Grand Opera House on Great Victoria Street is a living theatre; it too is dramatic in its late Victorian architectural intensity. Only two other theatres in Ireland survive from the same period, the Gaiety in Dublin and the Theatre Royal in Waterford. Almost opposite the Grand Opera House is another absolute gem, the late Victorian Crown Liquor Saloon. Its tiling and windows are extravagant; miraculously, the building has managed to survive the depredations of the years. The newest additions to the city are along the Lagan, including the new Waterfront Hall.

The highly stylised Odyssey Centre, which cost around stg £100 million to erect, is an impressive multi-purpose leisure and sports centre, and was completed in 2001.

DERRY

ONE DAY

See the two cathedrals, one Catholic, the other Church of Ireland, as well as the remarkable city walls. St Eugene's Catholic Cathedral was designed in 1853, but its last piece, the cross atop the spire, was not put in place until 1903. St Columb's Church of Ireland Cathedral dates from the 17th century and was the first cathedral built in these islands after the Reformation. The oldest Catholic church in Derry is the Long Tower Church, which dates from 1784–86 and has a fine rococo interior.

From Derry, travel 10 km (6 miles) west to Burt, Co. Donegal, to see the truly outstanding modern church designed by Liam McCormick, a noted architect from Derry. It's close to the Grianán Aileach, the circular prehistoric monument that was reconstructed in the 19th century. St Aengus Church is at the foot of the hill and prehistory provided lots of inspiration for the church, which is considered the finest post-Vatican II church in Ireland. The church is circular, with a stone-walled exterior. Inside, the soaring roof lantern is above the altar. The whole atmosphere is one of awe-inspiring serenity, a fitting place to end this architectural tour of Ireland.

TRAIL 7

The Yeats Trail

DUBLIN

ONE DAY

W.B. Yeats (1865–1939) was one of Ireland's greatest poets, a Nobel prizewinner, acclaimed in his own time. The four-day Yeats trail begins in Dublin, not Sligo, for it was in Dublin that Yeats was born. The house of his birth, 5 Sandymount Avenue, near the RDS, has a plaque on the outside, but as it is a private house the interior cannot be viewed. He spent the first three years of his life here, before his family moved to London for the next 14 years. However, W.B. Yeats often spent holidays with his grandparents, the Pollexfens, in Sligo, visits that had a profound influence on him and which he recalled in "Reveries Over Childhood and Youth".

After the family's return to Dublin, Yeats went to school at the High School at the top of Harcourt Street. The site is now occupied by the Dublin district headquarters of the Garda Síochána. Initially, the family lived at Island View, overlooking Howth Harbour, but in 1883 they moved to what is now 142 Harold's Cross Road.

His Dublin connections don't end there. In 1922, when he was made a senator in the new Irish Free State, he bought 82 Merrion Square, an elegant townhouse, where his Monday evening gatherings were models of artistic decorum. Oliver St John Gogarty called the time that Yeats lived in Merrion Square his "silk hat period".

In 1928, after leaving the Senate, he lived briefly at 42 Fitzwilliam Square, before moving out to Riversdale, a fine house at Ballyboden Road, Rathfarnham. This was his last home. At the time of writing, the future status of the house is uncertain, as developers propose to redevelop the site and it is uncertain whether the house can be preserved as an historic monument.

After a day exploring the Yeats locations in Dublin, travel to Sligo, about four hours by car or train.

SLIGO

TWO DAYS

Two full days can be spent exploring all the places in and around Sligo with Yeats connections. In the centre of Sligo, at Hyde Bridge across the Garavogue River, the Yeats Memorial Building has frequent exhibitions of material on W.B. Yeats.

Across the road from the Yeats Building is the Silver Swan, formerly the site of Pollexfen Mill, while in Stephen Street, just across the Hyde Bridge, the Niland Gallery and Museum has much memorabilia on W.B. Yeats, including the Nobel Prize presented to him in 1923. Also in Sligo, you can enjoy the Yeats Candle-Lit Supper at the Yeats Room in the Blue Willow Restaurant in Wine Street, Sligo. The evenings detail Yeats's connections with Sligo.

Yeats Memorial Building, *tel (071) 7142693; fax (071) 7142780; email info@yeats-sligo.com; website www.yeats-sligo.com.*

Blue Willow Restaurant, *Temple Street, Sligo;* (restaurant open May–Sept, bookings through North West Tourism *tel (071) 7161201*).

To the west of Sligo, the great expanse of strand at Rosses Point, a marvellous natural landscape, is where Yeats spent many of his childhood holidays. Dominating the area is Knocknarea mountain, surmounted by Queen Maeve's cairn, again the subject of many references by W.B. Yeats.

In Ballisodare, south Sligo, the Middleton house and the nearby salley gardens are equally renowned, from his poem "Down by the Salley Gardens". Just to the east of Sligo is Lough Gill, the most renowned of all the Yeatsian poetic locations. You can follow the nature trail through Dooney and the Slish or Sleuth woods, settings that inspired the "Fiddler of Dooney" and the "Stolen Child". You can also stroll through Hazelwood Park, a public park at the western end of Lough Gill. The most famous connection with Lough Gill is the small offshore island of Innisfree, the setting for perhaps the best-known of Yeats's poems, the "Lake Isle of Innisfree". Just south of here is Glencar waterfall, a spectacular waterfall that also features in his poetry.

To the north of Sligo is Lissadell House, home of the Gore-Booth family. Maud Gonne had family connections here and was the great love of Yeats's life.

Also north of Sligo, at Drumcliff in the grounds of the Church of Ireland, is Yeats's grave. He died in the south of France in 1939, but his body wasn't returned to Ireland for burial until 1948. His gravestone has the often repeated epitaph: "Cast a cold eye on life on death, horseman pass by." A small heritage centre in the grounds here was opened in 1999 and contains material on Yeats.

Lissadell House, *near Sligo; tel (071) 63150* (open daily in summer).

Yeats Heritage Centre, *Drumcliff, Co. Sligo; tel (071) 44956; fax (071) 40273; email info@drumcliffe.ie; website www.drumcliffe.ie* (open all year Mon–Fri 8.30am–6pm, Sat 10am–6pm, Sun 1pm–6pm).

GORT

ONE DAY

For the third and final part of this tour, travel 80 km (50 miles) south of Sligo to Gort, in east Co. Galway. W.B. Yeats had many connections with Lady Gregory, while both were closely associated with the Abbey Theatre in Dublin. The great house at Coole, Lady Gregory's home, is long gone, but you can still walk through the woods that inspired Yeats. The autographed tree is still there, with many famous literary signatures. You can also see the swans.

The new heritage centre at Coole has much material on W.B. Yeats. It's in the old stable yard at Coole and includes an audio-visual presentation. Drive 3 km (2 miles) from Coole to Thoor Ballylee, the old Norman tower house that he bought and restored after his marriage to George. He lived here from 1919 until 1928 and the exhibition has much material on his life and works, while the rooms in the castle have been well restored. The tower and grounds can be visited, and there's also an audio-visual presentation.

Also of interest in this immediate area is the Kiltartan Gregory Museum and Millenium Park, 3 km (1.5 miles) north of Gort, which has more material on Lady Gregory and inevitably on W.B. Yeats.

Coole Heritage Centre, *Coole, Co. Galway; tel (091) 631804* (open daily in summer, 9.30am–6.30pm).

Thoor Ballylee, *near Coole, Co. Galway; tel/fax (091) 631436* (open daily Easter–Sept; between Oct and April *tel (091) 563081*).

Kiltartan Gregory Museum, *near Gort, Co. Galway; tel (091) 632346* (open daily in summer; Sept and May, Sun only lpm–5pm).

Autographed tree, Coole Park, Co. Galway

51

TRAIL 8

Film Locations

Various locations around the country have become well known as the production locations for TV series and films. One of the best known is the Dingle Peninsula, where David Lean shot *Ryan's Daughter* in 1970.

DINGLE PENINSULA

ONE DAY

Ironically, there is little left to see of the film set, but the making of the film is still much talked about locally and visitors can also enjoy the spectacular scenery. The storyline of the film was a little far-fetched, but appeals to anyone of a romantic turn of mind. Rosy Ryan is the daughter of the local pub owner; she's about to get married to a local school teacher, Charles Shaughnessy, who has little interest in the physical side of their relationship. Rosy meets a British Army officer, Major Randolph Doryan, who is stationed in the village to monitor contacts between the IRA and their German allies – this was during the First World War. Rosy and the Major make love in the woods, but Michael, the village idiot, finds one of Rosy's buttons and the secret is out. The village mob attacks Rosy for collaborating with the enemy, strips her and cuts off her hair. The Major then finds that Rosy has called off the affair; he promptly blows himself up. The film concludes with Rosy and Charles leaving to set up a new life in Dublin. The film itself is full of cinematic clichés and is downright risible in places.

Sarah Miles played Rosy, while Robert Mitchum played the schoolteacher and Christopher Jones played the Major. A number of Irish actors, including Des Keogh, Niall Tobin and the late Philip O'Flynn of the Abbey, took part.

The village of Kirrary was built as a set, near Dingle, but nothing remains today. The spectacular beach scenes were shot at Inch and Coumeenoole strands near Dingle, while Barrow strand near Tralee was also used. There are regular bus tours of the Dingle peninsula locations used in the film, as well as plenty of background descriptions.

Dingle Tourist Information Office, *tel (066) 9151188 for details.*

CONG

TWO DAYS

From Dingle, travel up to Cong in Co. Mayo for even more detailed film history. *The Quiet Man*, one of whose producers was the late Lord Killanin, was directed by John Ford and released in 1952. Three of the "greats" of American cinema starred in the film, Maureen O'Hara, John Wayne and Barry Fitzgerald.

In the film, Sean Thornton returns from the US to his home village of "Innisfree". He wants to buy a cottage that's owned by a widow, Sarah Tillane. His family had lived there for seven generations but Mrs Tillane says that her family has been in Ireland since Norman times. He outbids "Red" Will Danaher for the cottage and to make matters worse, Thornton starts courting Danaher's sister. There is a great fight in the film between Thornton and Danaher over the dowry for Danaher's sister, Mary Kate. She does get together with Sean Thornton, while Danaher ends up courting Mrs Tillane. It's all hopelessly romantic, a rosy American view of old Ireland, but it's still a classic film.

The original cottage used in the film was at Maam Bridge and is now in ruins, but the replica, in Cong, is now the Quiet Man Heritage Centre. Here you can see all the newspaper clippings of the time, with such headlines as "Hollywood takes over village of Cong" and "Hollywood invades Maam Valley". The original horse harness and reins used in the film can be seen here, while there's a replica of the big bed used in the production. In the film, after Thornton and Mary Kate are married, she won't sleep with him until the dowry has been paid. But the bed collapses nevertheless and Michaeleen Og Flynn, the local matchmaker, sees the collapsed bed the next day and thinks it was caused by passion! All the interior scenes for the film were shot in the US but nearly all the external scenes were filmed in Cong, which doubled for the fictitious village of Innisfree. The Catholic church was used for the interior scenes in church, while the Church of Ireland church was used for the exterior scenes.

In the nearby river, some of the fight scenes were staged. The village pub, which featured in the film, was actually an old-fashioned grocery shop, now a gift shop. Other scenes were filmed at nearby Ashford Castle. A railway station near Tuam was used for the train scenes, while further afield some filming was done in Clifden, on Lettergesh beach at Killary Harbour and in the grounds of Kylemore Abbey. Even Thoor Ballylee, once a home to W.B. Yeats, was brought into the action, used for the sequence where the heroine throws off her stockings.

It's a very full itinerary that can usefully be spread over two days. For details on what to see and where to go: *Gerry Collins; tel (092) 46089 or website www.quiet-man.cong@iol.ie.* **Quiet Man Heritage Centre**, *Cong, Co. Mayo; tel (092) 46293* (open daily, 17 March–31 Ocober 10am–5pm). **Tourist Information Office**, *Cong, Co. Mayo; tel (092) 46542* (open March–Nov).

Avoca Handweavers, Avoca, Co. Wicklow

LIMERICK

ONE DAY

Also close to the west coast of Ireland, some of the settings for the *Angela's Ashes* film have been re-created in Limerick. When Alan Parker was shooting the film, he found that all the old slums of Limerick had been torn down – now they've been re-created as a heritage centre. The stables of a refurbished house in the city have been turned into an *Angela's Ashes* centre.

The set pieces include the downstairs kitchen, which in the film was flooded by an open drain in winter; however, the re-creation is aesthetically pleasing, without any of the original smells. The kitchen includes the range that was used in the film. The centre, in Limerick's Georgian district, also has material on the history of Limerick and photographs from the film. Details from the local Tourist Information Office.

Angela's Ashes Heritage Centre, *2 Pery Square, Limerick; (061) 314130.*
Tourist Information Office, *Limerick; tel (061) 317522.*

CO. WICKLOW

ONE DAY

In the eastern part of Ireland, two locations stand out, one in Co. Wicklow, the other in Co. Cork. The former is the attractive village of Avoca, where the final series of the popular *Ballykissangel* drama was filmed for BBC television in 2001. The first series was broadcast in 1996 and since then the series has gained followers all over the world. Visit such well-known landmarks as the Catholic church and Fitzgerald's pub. The village itself is small and can be very busy in summer with all the visitors interested in *Ballykissangel*.

Not connected to the TV series, but interesting to visit in the village is the Avoca Handweavers

Moby Dick's Pub sign, Youghal, Co. Cork

premises, considered the oldest working mill in Ireland. Its café is also well-known for its delicious home-baked food.

Well over 40 films and TV series have been shot in Wicklow, in addition to the numerous films and series made at Ardmore Studios in Bray. There's now a County Wicklow Film Location Trail, which loops through the many locations used over the years. The Wicklow Film Commission will suggest trails to follow the locations.

County Wicklow Film Commission, *tel (0404) 61732 or 087 2321292.*

Youghal

One Day

Youghal, Co. Cork, is one of the most attractive seaside towns in Ireland. In 1954 its waterfront doubled as a New England harbour for John Huston's film of the great whaling epic *Moby Dick*, in which Gregory Peck played Captain Ahab. While the set, that was designed to look like New Bedford, has long since been demolished, you will find plenty of material about the film in the appropriately named Moby Dick pub, right by the waterfront. Some 75 photographs taken when the film was being made are on show here and there are also scrapbooks of press cuttings and other material. The pub is run by Kevin and Paddy Linehan, who are great enthusiasts on the subject and will be happy to answer any questions you care to ask about the film production. Tourists come here from all over the world.

Moby Dick's Pub, *Youghal, Co. Cork; tel (024) 92756.*

For lots of information on other film and TV locations around Ireland contact: **The Screen Commission of Ireland**, *16 Eustace Street, Temple Bar, Dublin 2; tel (01) 672 7252; website www.screencommireland.com.*

For details of the locations used in Northern Ireland for recent film productions contact: **The Northern Ireland Film Commission**, *21 Ormeau Avenue, Belfast; tel (02890) 232444; fax (02890) 239918; email joanne@nifc.co.uk; website www.nifc.co.uk.*

TRAIL 9

James Joyce

DUBLIN

ONE DAY

Following the trail of James Joyce through Dublin is comparatively easy, even though it's nearly a century since he actually lived in the city. Born in 1882 he spent the first 22 years of life in Dublin and the remainder of his life, until he died in 1941, in exile in Trieste, Paris and Zurich. All through the long years away from Ireland he remembered Dublin with immaculate accuracy, even though he was totally unsentimental about the place, even calling it on one occasion the "Centre of Paralysis". Joyce used to claim, however, that he knew Dublin so well that if the city were destroyed, it could be rebuilt with entire accuracy, brick by brick, from his written works, especially Ulysses. Even though much of central Dublin has been re-developed since the 1960s, it's still possible to follow a fascinating Joyce trail through city and suburb. Joyce lived in something like 23 houses during his time in the city. Not all of them are listed here.

Start at Prince's Street, beside the GPO in O'Connell Street. The offices of the old Freeman's Journal used to be here, but the building was destroyed in the 1916 Easter Rising. Today Prince's Street has dull department-store architecture, not enticing to look at, but you can imagine the old newspaper offices where Leopold Bloom, an advertisement canvasser for the paper, once "worked".

Then take a number 10, 11 or 19 bus from O'Connell Street up to Dorset Street. Just at the corner of Dorset Street and Eccles Street is the Mater Private Hospital. A plaque on its facade notes that this site had been Number 7 Eccles Street, the fictitious home of Bloom.

Cross back over Dorset Street, go along Temple Street and into Great Denmark Street, where you'll find Belvedere College. It's set in a fine 18th-century mansion. Here Joyce studied between 1893 and 1898, and you can have a look at the interior, with its Venetian plasterwork and the medallion-encrusted staircase.

Belvedere College, *Denmark Street, Dublin; tel (01) 874 4795* (open in term time Sept–July).

The James Joyce Centre just off Great Denmark Street is in a restored 18th-century town house that was once the dancing academy of Professor Dennis J. Maginni. The reference library has a substantial amount of material referring to Joyce and his works, as well as material on Dublin. Exhibition rooms show frequent displays relating to Joyce, there is a well-stocked book-shop and the Ulysses tearooms.

The James Joyce Centre, *35 North Great George's Street, Dublin; tel (01) 878 8587; fax (01) 878 8488; email joyce-cen@iol.ie; website www.jamesjoyce.com* (open daily for tours of house; also daily walking tours of Joyce's north inner city).

Ormond Quay Hotel, Dublin

From here, go down to Lower Gardiner Street and into Railway Street, taking care as this isn't the most salubrious part of the city. Number 82 Railway Street is where Bella Cohen's brothel once stood. It was a key location on Bloom's travels around Dublin on 16 June 1904. This whole area was known as "Monte", a hotbed of prostitution in the late 19th and early 20th centuries, although today the problem is drugs. All the brothels, some frequented by the young Joyce himself, are long since gone.

Entrance to the National Library of Ireland, Dublin

From Railway Street, walk beside the River Liffey. The Ormond Quay Hotel has plaques commemorating the Joycean connection with the place.

Ormond Quay Hotel, *Upper Ormond Quay, Dublin; tel (01) 872 1811.*

On the opposite side of the river, at Number 15 Usher's Island, the house that Joyce used to set his short story "The Dead" has been bought by a barrister, Brendan Kielty, who plans to restore the house to its original state.

Retrace your footsteps to the city centre, this time the south city centre. In Duke Street, the old Bailey Restaurant has vanished in the name of redevelopment, but the door from Number 7 Eccles Street that once stood inside the restaurant can now be seen in the Joyce Museum in Sandycove.

Fortunately, Davy Byrne's pub, also in Duke Street, remains as it always was, a temple to the Joycean cult, where Bloom had a glass of Burgundy wine and a Gorgonzola cheese sandwich. You can still see the murals painted by Harry Salkeld, Brendan Behan's father-in-law.

Follow Bloom's trail across Dawson Street (where he helped a blind man cross the road), along Molesworth Street and into the National Library. Near here, Bloom has a near encounter with Blazes Boylan, his wife's lover.

Walk down Kildare Street into Nassau Street and go just round the corner, at the back of Trinity College. Sweny's Pharmacy is remarkably unchanged since Joyce's time. The interior is still as it was then, very atmospheric with its potions and phials. The distance of this total city walk is 9 km (6 miles).

National Library, *Kildare Street, Dublin; tel (01) 6030200* (open Mon–Wed 10am–9pm, Thurs–Fri 10am–5pm, Sat 10am–1pm).

Four other destinations have close connections to Joyce, but are located outside the city centre. If you drive or take a taxi or a number 15 bus to the suburb of Rathgar you will come to Brighton Square. It may be called a square but in fact it's a tri-angular shape. Number 41 is where James Joyce was born on 2 February 1882. You can see the exterior of the house, virtually unchanged from Joyce's time.

The James Joyce Tower in Sandycove can be reached either by number 8 bus from the city centre to Sandycove Road, or by the DART train to Dun Laoghaire. Sandycove is 12 km (7 miles) south-east of Dublin city centre.

The old Martello tower by the seafront was built in 1804 to guard against the threat of Napoleonic invasion. The first civilian tenant, in 1904, was Oliver St John Gogarty, wit, poet and surgeon. Joyce spent some time at the tower with Gogarty, and described it in the first chapter of Ulysses. Gogarty was transformed into the character of Buck Mulligan.

The tower now has an extensive Joyce museum and library. Among the items on display are first and rare editions of Joyce's work, letters and manuscript items, portraits and photographs of Joyce, his family and friends, and books about Joyce. Some of Joyce's personal possessions can be seen, including the waistcoat inherited from his father, his guitar, wallet, cigar case, cane and cabin trunk, as well as a tie from his wardrobe given to Samuel Beckett. Among recent acquisitions are a large relic of his former home at Millbourne Avenue, Drumcondra, now demolished, and an original issue of the Freeman's Journal describing Joyce's performance in the 1904 Feis Ceol.

James Joyce Museum and Library, *Sandycove, Co. Dublin; tel/fax (01) 280 9265: April–Oct; tel (01) 872 2077 and fax (01) 872 2231: Nov–March; email joycetower@dublintourism.ie* (open April–Oct, Mon–Sat l0am–5pm, Sun and public holidays 2pm–6pm. Closed for lunch on weekdays. Nov–March, by arrangement only).

The final out-of-city-centre stop on this odyssey is Sandymount Strand, which can be reached by the number 3 bus from the city centre, or by DART, as far as Sandymount station. It is 3 km (2 miles) from the city centre.

The long strand was cherished by Joyce and his beloved Nora Barnacle. When the tide goes out, the sands stretch far into the distance. The Martello tower, made famous on the very first Bloomsday celebrations held in 1954, has been spoiled with ugly metal shutters dating from its conversion into a restaurant (disused at the time of writing).

The journey round the Joyce sites in the city centre will take a full day, while visiting the suburban sites will take a further day. Two other Joycean locations, both outside Dublin, are worth mentioning.

In Mullingar, the Greville Arms Hotel has a small collection of Joyce-related material in honour of the writer's stay there, while at Galway the Nora Barnacle House is preserved. In this tiny one-up, one-down terrace house Nora Barnacle was brought up as a child.

Nora Barnacle House, *Bowling Green, Galway; (open daily). Details from: Ireland West Tourism, Galway; tel (091) 563081.*

Trail 10

Round Towers

Round towers dot the landscape of Ireland, relics of early Christian Ireland. These great stone-built towers, slim and pointing skywards, usually about 30 metres (100 ft) high, are the most distinctive pieces of architecture in Ireland. The round towers were built over a period of 300 years, starting in about AD 950 with a round tower at Slane, Co. Meath, and ending with the last round tower built in 1238 at Annaghdown, Co. Galway.

The round towers usually had several wooden floors and to reach the top, people had to climb a series of ladders from one floor to the next. One of the most accessible round towers that is wholly intact, with ladders for ascending to the top, is beside St Canice's Cathedral in Kilkenny city. Round towers were topped off with a conical roof. In all cases, entrances to round towers were raised well above ground level and could only be reached by ladder. This essential protective device was useful, especially during Viking times, when parts of the east and south coast were overrun with Viking invaders.

Altogether over 100 round towers were built in most parts of Ireland, and fortunately nearly 60 survive to the present day. They are grouped mainly in Dublin and Leinster, in the midlands and the south, while Northern Ireland has some too. Accordingly, trails have been grouped into these four distinctive regions.

Dublin and Leinster

Two Days

Begin your trail in Dublin. The suburb of Clondalkin, in west Dublin, has a well-preserved round tower literally by the side of the main street. It is built from limestone, has its cap in place and is in excellently preserved condition. The other round tower in Dublin, in the middle of Glasnevin cemetery, isn't authentic – it dates from the 19th century but is a very accurate reproduction.

From Dublin, travel north for 16 km (10 miles) to Swords, a bustling dormitory town. Just west of the town centre, in the grounds of St Columba's Church of Ireland, there's a well-preserved round tower standing 23 metres (75 ft) high in the verdant setting of the churchyard. It was built as part of a monastery said to have been founded by St Columba. The tower itself is built from rubble masonry. The belfry and the conical cap were rebuilt, clumsily, in the Middle Ages or later, but otherwise the tower is in good condition.

From Swords, travel 8 km (5 miles) north to the small market garden town of Lusk. At the entrance to the town, the medieval church has a round tower incorporated into the external fabric of the church. An added attraction here is that the church has been converted into a museum, open during the summer.

Glendalough, Co. Wicklow - view over Glendassan River to the Monastic City

From Lusk, return to the main N1 road and continue northwards for a further 35 km (29 miles) through the town of Drogheda to Monasterboice. This is one of the most spectacular settings for a round tower anywhere in Ireland, as the tower, largely preserved except for its top portion, is surrounded by a series of high crosses. Monasterboice was a site of deep religious significance, the site of a monastery founded by St Buithe, who died in 521. The most striking cross is the West Cross, which stands 7 metres (23 ft) high and has unusual carvings. The site also contains two ruined churches.

Continue 20 km (12 miles) north of Monasterboice, again on the N1, passing through the attractive village of Castlebellingham. Just past the village, and to the immediate left of the main road, Dromiskin village has a well-preserved round tower.

From here travel 45 km (27 miles) south-west along the R166, then the N52, through the town of Ardee, the agreeable market town of Kells. The town has great historical provenance, centred around St Columba's Church of Ireland, in a most atmospheric graveyard. Kells is famous for the Book of Kells, Ireland's most famous illuminated manuscript, depicting the Gospels. It was handwritten over a period of many years during the 8th century in the monastery at Kells. The original is still on display at Trinity College, Dublin, despite efforts by local people to have it returned to its place of origin. You can see a facsimile copy in the church. Just outside the church, you can see the fairly well-preserved round tower, which was built before 1075. It has lost its conical cap and the heads carved by the doorway have been badly disfigured by the weather, but otherwise it's in good structural condition.

For the second day of this tour of Leinster round towers, travel south from Dublin, towards Bray. About 16 km (10 miles) south of Dublin, just off the main N11 at Rathmichael, there's a well-preserved round tower. The real jewel, however, is further down the road, 40 km (24 miles) south-west of Dublin.

This is the round tower at Glendalough, perhaps the best known in Ireland and one of the most easily accessible. The whole group of monastic ruins is one of the most important historical sites in Ireland. Despite many raids by the Vikings and local people, the monastic community managed to survive. The whole site, which is accessed just at the rear of the hotel in the centre of the village, has a magnificent collection of early Christian buildings, including the cathedral and St Kevin's Church, the latter named in honour of the saint, born in AD 498, who came to this valley in search of solitude. The round tower, in the centre of the site, was built in either the 11th or 12th century, making it a late tower. This round tower stands 33 metres (108 ft) high and was originally built as a bell tower to summon the monks to prayer. It was also built for defensive purposes, with the entrance 3.6 metres (12 ft) above ground level. The structure is in good condition and the cone was restored in the late 19th century.

From Glendalough, travel 25 km (15 miles) across the barren but spectacular landscapes of the Wicklow Gap – it's one of the best drives in Ireland – to the village of Hollywood. From here, take the R411/413 as far as the village of Kilcullen, also the site of a round tower (12 km/7 miles).

Continue from the village of Kilcullen for 8 km (5 miles) to Kildare town, for another magnificent round tower. In the grounds of the 19th-century Church of Ireland cathedral, which is a restoration of a 13th-century building, the round tower stands 30 metres (98 ft) high. It has been substantially restored and is open to the public. You can climb the internal ladders to the top for magnificent views across the Curragh plain.

From Kildare, travel to Portlaoise on the main N7, then turn off for Timahoe, a distance altogether of 40 km (24 miles). Timahoe village has a broad green; you can see the memorial here to the visit by a former US president, the late Richard Nixon, in 1974. His Quaker ancestors came from Timahoe. Beside the green is a magnificent round tower, 33 metres (108 ft) high, with a Romanesque double doorway. This tower is unusual, as it leans slightly, about 0.6 metres (2 ft) from the perpendicular.

From Timahoe, travel south for 40 km (24 miles) on the R430 then the N78, through Castlecomer, to the best round tower of this section, in Kilkenny city.

St Canice's medieval Church of Ireland Cathedral is a magnificent building, dating from the 13th century. Its early Gothic style has been substantially restored at different periods. The cathedral is the second longest in Ireland and has many fine interior architectural features. Outside, just beside the entrance door, is the round tower, built before AD 1000, standing 30 metres (98 ft) high and perfectly preserved. You can climb a series of almost vertical ladders, from floor to floor, until you emerge on the roof. It's a dizzy prospect and is not recommended to anyone who suffers from heights, but the views across this medieval city are priceless; this is the best vantage point in Kilkenny.

MIDLANDS

ONE DAY

Begin this tour in Roscrea, Co. Tipperary. Roscrea is an exceptionally interesting town, not least for the 18th-century Damer House. It also has St Cronan's Church, which stands on the site of a monastery founded in the early 7th century. Near the ruins and very accessible from the main N7 road is the round tower. It was built in the 8th century and stands just 18 metres (60 ft) high. The conical cap came off in the 12th century and the top 6 metres (20 ft) was knocked off in the fighting of 1798.

Round Tower, Clonmacnois monastery, Co. Offaly

From Roscrea, drive north for 45 km (27 miles) through Birr to the medieval ecclesiastical site of Clonmacnois, one of the most important in Ireland. The monastery here, overlooking the River Shannon, was founded by St Kieran in AD 545. The round tower forms a striking part of the collection of buildings. It may have been built in the 10th century and although it has lost its conical cap, it is otherwise in well-preserved condition.

THE SOUTH

ONE DAY

Two sites are well worth visiting for their round towers and they can be easily visited in a day.

At Ardmore in west Waterford, the

round tower stands 29 metres (95 ft) high, has four storeys and a cap. The corbels that mark each storey are carved with human and other representations. In recent years, the round tower has been restored, so that once again, it's in perfect condition. Not only is it one of the best round towers anywhere in Ireland, but its setting on the heights above Ardmore village, overlooking the bay, is truly magnificent.

From Ardmore, drive 45 km (27 miles) along the N25, through Youghal and Midleton, to Cloyne, a small village close to the eastern shores of Cork harbour. The cathedral here dates from the 14th century and close by is the Cloyne round tower, which dates from the 10th century and stands 30 metres (100 ft) high. It can be climbed by visitors.

NORTHERN IRELAND

ONE DAY

Undoubtedly the best preserved round tower in the North is in Antrim town, 20 km (12 miles) north-east of Belfast. This round tower stands among the trees in Steeple Park; it dates back to around AD 900 and is all that is left of an ancient monastery founded in the 6th century and abandoned in the 12th century. The round tower itself has been well preserved and the conical cap has been replaced; it is 27 metres (90 ft) high.

From Antrim, drive 60 km (37 miles) north, through Ballymena, to the village of Armoy. It is a very attractively set village, on the River Bush and close to Ballycastle forest. The round tower here is only partially preserved, standing just 11 metres (35 ft) tall.

Northern Ireland is the least populated part of Ireland in terms of round towers, with only seven in all. One of the best known is at Devinish Island in Fermanagh lakeland, which is 26 metres (85 ft) high. It is in a very complete state, has finely built masonry and, unusual for any Irish round tower, has sculptured ornaments.

TRAIL 11

Battle Sites

Some memorable battles that reshaped Irish history can still be traced today, and the course of the battles on the sites where they happened can be followed on this six-day trail. One of the most outstanding battles, yet one of the least known, is the Battle of Aughrim which took place in July 1691.

AUGHRIM

ONE DAY

The village of Aughrim is on the main N6 Dublin–Galway road, 6 km (4 miles) west of Ballinasloe, Co. Galway. The village itself is pleasant and has a heritage centre detailing the progress of the Battle of Aughrim. Following the actual course of the battle on the original landscape will take one day.

The origins of the Battle of Aughrim date back to the great wars in Europe in the 1680s. Louis XIV, the Sun King of France, was at war with his Continental neighbours. Ironically, the Pope was on the side of the Catholic Sun King's enemies, who included William of Orange. He was married to his first cousin, Mary, the daughter of the last King from the House of Stuart, James II.

James II was a converted Catholic, married to a Protestant. He was tolerated on the condition that Mary would succeed him. However, James's second wife gave birth to a son and potential Catholic. It was even rumoured at the time that a baby boy was smuggled into the Queen's bedroom in a warming pan as part of a Popish plot to ensure a Catholic heir. James eventually fled England.

The Dutch King William later came to claim the throne of England. He and his wife Mary became the only joint monarchs in English history.

James decided to use Ireland as a stepping stone and war developed between his forces and those of his son-in-law, William. The war in Ireland began with the arrival of King James at Kinsale on 12 March 1689. The decisive turning point took place at Aughrim two years later. In between came three famous Williamite victories, at Derry, Enniskillen and the Boyne. The Battle of the Boyne was a mere skirmish compared to Aughrim – on the Boyne battle site, one in sixty of the soldiers died, whereas at Aughrim, the figure was one in five. More people died in Aughrim than the combined totals of Clontarf (1014), Kinsale (1601), the Boyne (1690), Vinegar Hill (1798) and the 1916 Easter Rising. More soldiers died at Aughrim in one afternoon than were killed in the three-day Battle of Gettysburg in the American Civil War.

The French commander at Aughrim was Lt. Gen. Charles Chalmont, the Marquis de Saint Ruhe or St Ruth as he is often called. He was no saint, being notorious for his treatment of Huguenots in France. Having landed with his forces at Limerick in May 1691, St Ruth and his forces proceeded to Athlone, where the Jacobite army was garrisoned under Patrick Sarsfield. After losing the Siege of Athlone, St Ruth had to decide whether to retreat to Limerick, await the arrival of the French fleet and face humiliation when he returned to France, or make a last desperate stand. He decided on the latter course of action, at Aughrim, the small village he had previously seen on his way from Limerick to Athlone.

The Battle of Aughrim was an almighty confrontation, so much so that it could be heard 56 km (35 miles) away in Galway. The 20,000 men of the Jacobite forces fought the 25,000 men on the Williamite side and a total of 9,000 were killed. There are no military graveyards at Aughrim; the bodies were simply left where they fell as a warning against further rebellion. The flock of sheep grazing upon the great hill of Eachroim was in fact the bleached skeletons of the fallen soldiers. Ginkel, the Williamite commander, offered sixpence for every weapon gathered, but had to reduce the payment to twopence because so much weaponry was gathered up.

St Ruth himself was killed at the crucial point of the battle, decapitated by chainshot (two cannonballs linked by a length of chain). When he fell, just on the verge of the only Jacobite victory in the war, the morale of his army crumbled.

In another instance of bad luck, 300 musketeers positioned near the ruins of Aughrim Castle ran out of ammunition and had to use their uniform buttons as makeshift bullets. The one cavalry regiment that was meant to be defending the Jacobite left flank abandoned the battle site when their commander, Henry Luttrell, left after being bribed by the Williamites. His reward was Luttellstown Castle, which still stands today at Castleknock just outside Dublin, and is now a luxury hotel.

With the collapse of the Jacobite forces, and the subsequent flight to the Continent of the "Wild Geese", Ireland's resistance to ruthless, steely British and Protestant rule was left without leadership. A stringent penal code was enacted in 1695 and by the middle of the following century, the amount of land held by Catholics fell to a mere 5 per cent.

In terms of Irish history, the Battle of Aughrim was a decisive turning point, with effects that have lasted to this day, and it was even more significant than the Battle of the Boyne. Perhaps the greatest irony of all is that the Pope had supported William of Orange in his campaign, a curious turn of history that is often forgotten.

In the Battle of Aughrim Heritage Centre, you can follow the events of 12 July 1691 in audio-visual format. The battlefield is laid out in miniature. Story panels tell the complex history of the period of the so-called Glorious Revolution. It is very detailed, but is told in easy-to-follow terms.

Apart from the centre, you can walk the site of the battlefield using the map provided. You can see the Pass of Urraghry, where the Williamite army made its first advance; St Ruth's fort, where the Jacobite commander observed his forces; and St Ruth's bush, where he was killed. You can also see the North Pass, where the Williamite forces reached the Jacobite defences. Today, the last great battle site on Irish soil is tranquil, a spot where you can ponder peacefully on the might-have-beens of Irish history.

Battle of Aughrim Heritage Centre, *Aughrim, Co. Galway; tel (0905) 73939; out of season (091) 509000* (open June–Sept, Tues–Sat l0am–6pm, Sun 2 pm–6pm).

ATHLONE

ONE DAY

From Aughrim, travel to Athlone, a distance of 30 km (18 miles) to see Athlone Castle, the scene of the great siege, part of this same campaign. Athlone Castle will take one day's exploration, also taking in the town centre and riverside sights of Athlone.

The town was besieged twice. The first time was in 1690, when 10,000 Williamite troops under General James Douglas besieged Athlone, held by a Jacobite force under the Governor of Athlone, Colonel Richard Grace. He refused to surrender and the town held out for a week. Grace was said to have remarked that he would defend the town until he had eaten his old boots. In terms of actual fighting, the siege in 1690 was hardly a proper siege at all.

Much worse was to come after a year of comparative peace, when in June 1691 the town was once again besieged by Williamite forces. This time the Williamite army had almost 25,000 men, under the Dutch General Godard de Ginkel.

The Williamites quickly captured the part of Athlone that is on the Leinster side of the River Shannon. The Jacobites broke down the bridge across the river and under the direction of their commander, St Ruth (later killed at Aughrim), they resisted all attempts at repairing it. A brave Sergeant of Dragoons, called Custume, lost his life attempting to dislodge the repair works of the Williamite soldiers. In so doing, he became a folk hero, celebrated in poetry and song and today's military barracks in Athlone are named after him. Then Ginkel's forces fired 12,000 cannonballs into the Connacht side of Athlone, badly damaging the castle and reducing many other buildings to ruin. The Williamite forces discovered a fording point on the river, crossed over and captured the castle.

Following the sieges, Athlone became the home of a permanent military garrison in 1697, and until 1970 the castle was an integral part of the barracks. Inside the castle, you can see an audio-visual presentation on the two sieges, as well as the subsequent military history of the town. From the time that Irish troops were first sent on a UN peacekeeping mission to the Congo in 1960, they have been involved in many UN operations around the world. This modern peacekeeping involvement is also described in the castle. There's a third facet to the castle's historical records, the life story of Count John McCormack (1884–1945), the world-famous tenor, who was born in Athlone, just across the river from the castle.

Athlone Castle, *Athlone, Co. Westmeath; tel (0902) 72107/92912* (open daily May–Sept).

For further information: **Athlone Tourist Information Office**, *in Athlone Castle, tel (0902) 94630.*

BATTLE OF THE BOYNE

ONE DAY

The third great battle site is of the Battle of the Boyne, near Drogheda, 48 km (30 miles) north of Dublin. Touring the battle site and the town of Drogheda will take one day.

By the time the Battle of the Boyne took place on 12 July 1690, the war in Ireland had been going on for a year. King William himself arrived in Belfast in June 1690, with a further 15,000 reinforcements, bringing the strength of his forces to 36,000.

King James had retreated from the North, where he had failed to take either Derry or Enniskillen. If he wanted to hold Dublin, he had to make the River Boyne his line of defence. So by the end of June 1690, James had his 25,000-strong Jacobite army camped by the side of the Boyne. By the time the battle was concluded, about 500 Williamite solders and 1,000 Jacobite men had been killed. William won control over Dublin and half of Leinster – James fled to Dublin and within three weeks of the battle, was ensconced in France.

Today, you can see King William's Glen, on the eastern edge of the Townley estate, about 6 km (4 miles) west of Drogheda. The glen, extending for about 1.6 km (1 mile), was used by part of the Williamite army to conceal its approach to the Boyne. From the viewing platform, you can see the layout of the battlefield. There's a small information centre in a portakabin, which has plenty of detail available on the site. Plans exist to build a full-scale heritage centre here.

Battle of the Boyne Information Centre, *near Drogheda, Co. Louth; tel (041) 9841644* (open daily during the summer).

The battle itself is commemorated every year in the North, at the so-called Sham Fight in the grounds of Scarva House, Scarva, Co. Down, on 13 July annually.

In the meantime, back in the Boyneside town of

Drogheda, the new Drogheda Heritage Centre has a fine audio-visual presentation on 800 years of the town's history. This includes Cromwell's bloody siege of Drogheda in 1649, when his forces killed 2,000 of the town's inhabitants and sent most of the survivors to Barbados. This audio-visual display has a substantial element on the Battle of the Boyne.

Drogheda Heritage Centre, *Drogheda, Co. Louth; tel (041) 9836643 or 087 2305698; email reillytom@eircom.net* (open Tues–Sat 10am–5pm, Sun 2pm–6pm, all year).

DERRY

ONE DAY

The precursor to Aughrim and the Battle of the Boyne was the Siege of Derry in 1689. Early in the 17th century, the city and much of the surrounding land had been granted by James I to the City of London, hence the name subsequently used, Londonderry. A large colony of Protestants was imported. The walls surrounding the town were completed in 1618 and are still extant today.

Various sieges of Derry took place during the 17th century, but none was so spectacular or as famous as the one of 1689. The town's garrison and a large number of Protestants who had fled there from other parts of the North took refuge in Derry. The invading Jacobite army threw a boom across the River Foyle at Culmore, preventing food ships from reaching the city. Several thousand people within the walls died from starvation and disease. On 28 July the boom was forced aside by the Mountjoy, one of the English convoy that relieved the city. The siege had lasted 105 days.

Today, when you are walking the walls, you can see many of the cannons used during the 1689 siege. The largest is Roaring Meg, near the Double Bastion, which played a prominent part in defending the city. Guided tours of the walls take place daily between June and September, starting at the Tourist Information Office. The Tower Museum in the city centre has much material on the history of Derry.

Details of guided tours of the walls are available from the **Tourist Information Office**, *44 Foyle Street, Derry; tel (02871) 267284.*

Enniskillen Castle, Co. Fermanagh

Tower Museum, *Union Hall Place, Derry; tel (02871) 372411* (open daily July–Aug, Tues–Sat, bank holidays Sept–June).

At St Columb's Church of Ireland Cathedral, at the top of Bishop Street, beyond the Diamond, you can see stained-glass windows depicting the great siege of 1689. The keys of the gates which were closed against the Jacobites are on show in the chapterhouse, while the 1633 cathedral also has audio-visual shows on the siege.

St Columb's Church of Ireland Cathedral, *Bishop Street, Derry; tel (02871) 267313* (open daily, all year).

Related to the events in Derry is the story of the Ulster

Plantation, Hugh O'Neill and the Flight of the Earls. The Plantation of Ulster Visitor Centre, 45 km (27 miles) south-east of Derry, tells the story through interactive display and an audio-visual show.

The Plantation of Ulster Visitor Centre, *50 High Street, Draperstown, Co. Derry; tel (02879) 627800* (open daily, all year).

Back in Derry, you can see much more recent evidence of battles at the entrance to the Bogside, where the Battle of the Bogside happened in August 1969. The slogan "You are now entering Free Derry" is perhaps the most famous to emerge from the city. Hundreds of local people battled to prevent incursions into the Bogside district by police and army and it was an inevitable follow-on from the events of the previous 5 October, when civil rights marchers in the Waterside were baton-charged by the RUC, an incident that was seen on the world's TV screens and gave the first internationalised inkling of what was to come during the subsequent 30 years of "Troubles".

BENBURB AND CALEDON

ONE DAY

Benburb, 10 km (6 miles) north-west of Armagh city, was the site of the great battle in 1646 when the Irish army led by Owen Roe O'Neill defeated the English and Scottish forces of General Munro. It was a continuation of the uprising against the planters, or the colonisers of Ulster, that had begun in 1641 and which continued until Cromwell's bloody campaign in 1649. Today in Benburb, you can visit the early 17th-century Plantation Benburb Castle, high above the River Blackwater. It stands in the grounds of the Servite Priory. At the Priory, you can also inspect the history of the O'Neills.

The Benburb Valley Heritage Centre, set in a 19th-century weaving factory beside the old Ulster Canal, not only tells the story of linen making, but appropriately for these battle themes, has a scale model of the Battle of Benburb.

Benburb Castle, *Benburb, Co. Armagh; tel (02837) 548241* (visits by arrangement).

Benburb Valley Heritage Centre, *Milltown Road, Benburb, Co. Armagh; tel (02837) 549885* (open daily, Easter–Sept or by arrangement).

ENNISKILLEN

ONE DAY

Enniskillen is 75 km (46 miles) south-west of Benburb. The town was settled by English and Scottish colonists after the charter granted by James I in 1613. During the wars of 1641 it was held for a time by the royalists, but finally surrendered to the Parliamentary forces of Sir Charles Coote. In 1689, almost simultaneously with the Siege of Derry, Enniskillen was one of the main strongholds in Ulster of the English and Scottish settlers. Attacking Jacobite forces were repulsed several times.

Today, you can see these events and all the other great historical events of town and county in Enniskillen Castle, which was originally a stronghold of Gaelic chieftains. Parts of the castle date back to the 17th century.

Enniskillen Castle, *Enniskillen, Co. Fermanagh; tel (02866) 325000* (open daily all year).

TRAIL 12

The Goldsmith Trail

MIDLANDS

ONE DAY

Oliver Goldsmith (1728–1774) was one of London's most distinguished 18th-century dramatists, author of such renowned comedies as School for Scandal. After 1752 Goldsmith spent his life outside Ireland, firstly in mainland Europe, returning to London in 1756. However, despite all his travels and his long years living away from Ireland, he always remained true to the country of his birth and upbringing.

A trail through a carefully delineated area near Athlone in central Ireland gives a good insight into the early life of Goldsmith, who was born at Pallas in Co. Longford, where his father was the Church of Ireland rector supplementing his income by farming. When Goldsmith was 2 years of age, the family moved to Lissoy in Co. Westmeath, where his father was appointed to the Church of Ireland. His formative years were spent here and these experiences shaped the emotional ties that were to find expression in "The Deserted Village".

One of his most famous poems, this was set in the village of Sweet Auburn, which in real life is Lissoy, on the road from Ballymahon to Athlone. In the centre of the village, which also featured in She Stoops to Conquer, is the Three Jolly Pigeons pub. At the entrance to the pub, you can see the millstone from the village mill, mentioned in "The Deserted Village", regarded as one of the best pastoral poems in the English language. The millstone came from the Busy Mill nearby, which was in use until 1860. Today nothing remains of the mill except ruins and the babbling brook. Also in Lissoy, you can see the sites of the original Ale House and the Hawthorn Bush. The site of the old schoolhouse, mentioned in the poem, can also be seen.

When the family lived in Lissoy parsonage, the young Goldsmith, standing at his front door, could see Kilkenny West Church on a hill in the distance; that was the church of which his father was rector. When, in "The Deserted Village",

Goldsmith refers to "The church that top't the neighbouring hill", Goldsmith's heart must have been back in Lissoy. Legend has it that Goldsmith's literary career began when he was very young, in the church when his father was preaching. He noticed a rat climbing down a rope from the belfry and immediately composed the following line: "A pious rat, for want of stairs, came down a rope to say his prayers."

Another village in this area with a Goldsmith connection is Ardagh, often voted Ireland's tidiest village in the Tidy Towns competition. It is 10 km (6 miles) south-east of Longford.

Here a famous prank was played on the young Goldsmith in 1744, when he was 16 years old and travelling from his school of Edgeworthstown to his home in Lissoy. Night was falling, Goldsmith had a guinea in his pocket, so he decided to take shelter in an inn. A local wag called Kelly pointed out the Big House, the mansion of Sir George Fetherston, and said it was the inn. The lady of the manor took up the prank when Goldsmith knocked at the front door. Goldsmith remembered the incident and it became the inspiration for his classic play She Stoops to Conquer, which he had originally called The Mistakes of a Night. The Big House is now St Brigid's Training Centre. Material on Goldsmith's connections with Ardagh can be seen in the heritage centre.

Heritage Centre, *Ardagh, Co. Longford; tel (043) 75277* (open daily).

Goldsmith lived at nearby Ballymahon for three years before emigrating in 1752, never to return to Ireland. In 1999, a life-sized sculpture by Eamonn O'Doherty on the theme "The Traveller" was unveiled in Main Street, Ballymahon. A Goldsmith Summer School is held in this district every year, usually in June.

Goldsmith Summer School; *details from John O'Donnell, Rathmore, Ballymahon, Co. Longford; tel (0902) 32374, (087) 2286611.*

At Goldsmith's birthplace, Pallas, a mould of the famous statue by John Foley in Trinity College, Dublin, has been erected. The Church of Ireland at Forgney, 4 km (2.5 miles) south-east of Ballymahon, has a memorial window to Goldsmith.

TRAIL 13

The Easter Rising

DUBLIN

ONE DAY

The Easter Rising, which began in the General Post Office in O'Connell Street, Dublin on Easter Monday, 24 April 1916, was the seminal event of modern Irish history. From that one single event, when a group of rebels seized the GPO and declared Ireland a Republic, all subsequent modern Irish history has flowed. This includes the setting up of the Irish Free State, which was declared a Republic in 1949, the partitioning of Ireland and the formation of Northern Ireland in 1920 as a separate six-county State.

Initially, public reaction to the Rising was hostile and the rebels had little support. It was a sunny Easter Monday and people were at the Fairyhouse Races, just north of Dublin, enjoying themselves, when the news filtered through. However, pockets of insurrection started all over Dublin and within a couple of days the battle was on. The British authorities decided to take a tough stance, arrested the leaders of the Rising when they surrended a week later, tried them

St Enda's Pearse Museum, Rathfarnham, Dublin

arbitrarily and then executed fifteen of them, including Patrick Pearse, the man who declared the Republic, and James Connolly, a labour leader, who had been injured in the fighting. He was shot dead as he sat in a wheelchair. Typical reaction came from the leader in the Irish Independent, which declared that the authorities should take tough action against the rebel leaders. That was merely a reflection of popular sentiment, but the feeling soon changed.

The execution of the fifteen was a monumental blunder by the British government; within two years, the old Irish Party at Westminster, which had supported constitutional reform leading to home rule, had been swept out of existence and in the general election two years after the Easter Rising, Sinn Féin won 73 seats at Westminster, which they didn't take. In 1919, the Dáil (lower house of the Irish Parliament) was declared, illegally, at a meeting in the Mansion House in Dublin city centre. The Provisional Government came into being.

That same year, the first shots were fired in the War of Independence, when two members of the Royal Irish Constabulary were ambushed and shot at a quarry in Soloheadbeg in Co. Tipperary. The War of Independence raged until 1921, when the Anglo-Irish Treaty was signed and the Irish Free State came into being.

Number 27, Pearse Street – this is where it all began. A plaque stands outside the house (then in Brunswick Street) where the brothers Patrick and Willie Pearse were brought up. Their father, who came from Birmingham, had run a successful stonemason's business here for many years and the family lived on the premises. The young Patrick was an idealist and poet, committed not only to freedom for Ireland but also to the Irish language.

The house was built in the 1820s. It is the only house left belonging to the 1916 leaders and it has been restored to the condition and style it was in the early 20th century, when it was still home to the Pearse brothers.

Number 27, *Pearse Street, Dublin; for details, contact the Dublin Civic Trust, 4 Castle Street, Dublin 2; tel (01) 475 6911.*

From the city centre, take the number 16 bus or drive the 10 km (6 miles) to Rathfarnham.

St Enda's, Rathfarnham, is a finely restored house that was once occupied by the school run by Patrick Pearse. The house has been turned into a museum, with many letters and other artefacts relating to Pearse and his ideals, while you can also see an audio-visual presentation. A visit to St Enda's will give a good insight into the type of man Pearse was and why he became certain that the Easter Rising, a blood sacrifice for the Irish nation, was the only way to proceed to Irish freedom. The house is set in a park.

St Enda's, *Grange Road, Rathfarnham, Dublin 16; tel (01) 493 4208; fax (01) 493 6120* (open daily, all year).

Return to the city centre where you can see several locations that figured prominently in the Easter Rising. At the College of Surgeons on St Stephen's Green and around the Green as far as the Shelbourne Hotel, rebel troops set up barricades and firing positions. Among those taking part in the Rising at this location was Countess Markievicz – she was to become the first-ever female minister in an Irish government.

Also on the southside of the city, you can see where the old Jacob's biscuit factory once stood in Aungier Street. A college of the Dublin Institute of Technology now stands on the site and there are no plaques. Another south-side site, which is marked by a plaque on the exterior walls, is the office block that was Bolands Mills. In 1916, this was a big flour mill held by Eamon de Valera and the rebels. De Valera and his men heroically defended the mill to the bitter end, but they had to surrender. He was the only 1916 leader not to be executed, because he was technically an American citizen. He went on to become arguably the greatest Irish politician of the 20th century. In recent years the building has been converted into a modern office block, so no trace of the original building remains.

Nearby is Mount Street Bridge, where 2,000 troops coming in from the boat at Kingstown (now Dun Laoghaire) to help quell the Rising were ambushed.

From Bolands Mills, walk the short distance or take a bus along Pearse Street back into the city centre, about 2 km (1 mile). The GPO, the heart of the Rising, is unmistakeable in O'Connell Street. The building was originally designed in a neoclassical style by Francis Johnston and was opened in 1815.

Interior of Kilmainham Jail, Dublin

The Irish Volunteers held it for a week of the Rising, during which time it came under substantial bombardment. The building was so badly damaged that restoration wasn't completed, and the building reopened to the public, until 1929. Inside the present-day building you can admire the famous bronze sculpture of the dying Cúchulainn, a leader of the Red Branch Knights in Celtic mythology. The statue was the work of Raymond Sheppard and was unveiled in 1935. Surrounding the statue are various paintings depicting the Rising.

Patrick Pearse was deeply influenced by ancient Gaelic literature and mythology, so the legend of Cúchulainn is deeply symbolic. During the Easter Rising, not only was the GPO virtually destroyed, but so too was Sackville Street (the old name for O'Connell Street). Many buildings in the street, including Clerys department store directly opposite, were also badly damaged and the damage extended into streets running off O'Connell Street, including North Earl Street and Henry Street.

During the early 1920s, a massive reconstruction programme took place. The old-style Liberty Hall on Eden Quay, which was also badly damaged, is now the site of the towering modern Liberty Hall, a symbol for trade union power. The British forces had stationed a gunboat, the Helga, on the River Liffey, a short distance from the city centre and the shells from this ship caused an immense amount of damage.

From the city centre, take the number 518, 78A or 79 bus from Aston Quay to Kilmainham Jail on Inchicore Road, 3 km (2 miles) from the city centre. (Car parking is difficult in the vicinity of the jail.) Kilmainham Jail lives up to its grim, forbidding reputation. This prison was opened in 1796 and was first used to house prisoners from the 1798 Rebellion. Three more rebellions took place during the 19th century, in 1803, 1848 and 1867, and the leaders of those uprisings, including Robert Emmet and Thomas Francis Meagher, were imprisoned here. So too was Charles Stewart Parnell, one of Ireland's great constitutional leaders. In the immediate aftermath of 1916, the leaders captured in the GPO and elsewhere were held here. The tour and the presentation will give a good insight into 200 turbulent years of Irish history, while you can visit the cells and see the prison yard where the 1916 leaders, including Patrick Pearse and James Connolly, were executed.

Kilmainham Jail, *Inchicore Road, Dublin; tel (01) 453 5984* (open daily, April–Sept; Oct–March, Sun).

From Kilmainham to Arbour Hill is about 3 km (2 miles) as the crow flies, on the other side of the River Liffey. To get to Arbour Hill, take the number 37, 39 or 70 bus from the city centre.

Arbour Hill cemetery is directly behind the extension to the National Museum in Benburb Street. In the cemetery here, the fourteen men executed after the 1916 Rising are buried. The burial place is simple but formal, with the names of the dead leaders and the wording of the Proclamation carved in stone.

Arbour Hill Cemetery, *Arbour Hill, Dublin;* (open daily, admission free).

Return to the city centre, to Parnell Square, 1 km (0.6 miles) north of the GPO.

Garden of Remembrance, Dublin

The Garden of Remembrance, a large sunken garden close to the Writers Museum in Parnell Square, was designed in the early 1960s by Daithi Hanly, then Dublin city architect, and opened for the 1966 commemorations of the 50th anniversary of the Rising. The garden is peaceful and tranquil, where visitors are encouraged to reflect on all those who gave their lives for Irish freedom. The centrepiece is a large sculpture by Oisin Kelly, based on the theme of the Children of Lir.

Garden of Remembrance, *Parnell Square, Dublin;* (open daily, admission free).

Useful reading on the Easter Rising would be the 1916 Proclamation, which can be freely purchased and has glorious and uplifting ideals, not always maintained in the "grocer's republic" that came into being afterwards. Another useful source is *The Irish Times Handbook of the 1916 Rebellion*, available in the National Library of Ireland, Kildare Street, Dublin.

TRAIL 14

Healthy and Holy Wells

All over Ireland, sacred holy wells are still revered and some of them still have annual processions. They are all in very disparate locations, widely separated, so it's best to see them as part of another tour, rather than taking an odyssey round Ireland simply in search of holy wells. With some five hundred to choose from, there's no shortage.

LISDOONVARNA

ONE DAY

Lisdoonvarna is a popular spa town founded in 1845, the only one remaining as such in Ireland, and is set just 8 km (5 miles) from the sea in the hilly Burren country of north Co. Clare.

The waters of Lisdoonvarna come from sulphurous and chalybeate (iron) springs, all of which have the valuable therapeutic element of iodine. The waters, especially the sulphur waters, are said to owe their efficacy to their radioactive properties. The main sulphur spring is on the southside of the town, while the main iron springs are on the northside. Visitors can take the waters at the Spa Centre. Facilities here include restroom, sauna baths and cafe.

Spa Centre, *Lisdoonvarna, Co. Clare; tel (065) 7074023* (open daily, June–Sept).

INISHMORE, ARAN ISLANDS

ONE DAY

St Kieran's Well, Inishmore, Aran Islands is one of the most strikingly set holy wells anywhere in Ireland; there's little to see but the setting is fantastic. However, Inishmore has many other points of interest, including the ruins of Dun Aengus.

MIDLANDS

ONE DAY

St Lazerian's Well, Old Leighlin, Co. Carlow is 14 km (9 miles) south of Carlow. The 12th-century cathedral, now Church of

Ireland, was much rebuilt in the 16th century. While the cathedral is of considerable interest to antiquarians, so too is the holy well, close to the cathedral but in Catholic hands.

St Lazerian's Well is named after the saint of the same name who lived in the 6th century and who is known locally as Molaise. Legend has it that when Molaise was building the original church here, the workmen were fed with a mysterious bullock, which was killed each evening for their supper. The next morning, the bullock reappeared. Molaise warned the workmen not to break any bones in the bullock, otherwise great harm would befall them. One evening, one of the workmen did break a bone in one of the bullock's legs, but denied responsibility. The next morning, he was covered in ulcers. He asked Molaise for forgiveness. Molaise took compassion on the man, and it's said that where they stood, the well sprung up. Molaise told the workman that if he bathed nine times in the water, his ulcers would disappear. He did and they vanished.

Celtic cross and ruins, Clonmacnois

The well itself was repaired nearly 80 years ago to improve the flow of water. However, to stop cattle polluting the water, the well was closed up – it remains closed, but water issues forth from a spout.

Up to two centuries ago, pattern days were very popular events at this well, but they became so disorderly that the local bishop prohibited them in 1810. (Pattern days were communal visits to holy wells under the protection of local patron saints. People on these visits often left coins, flowers and pieces of cloth as tokens of their gratitude.) These days, on the saint's day, an ecumenical procession is held to the well, when local Catholic and Protestant communities take part. The well is always accessible and is free.

From Old Leighlin, drive 50 km (31 miles) north, through Carlow and Athy, to Kildare town. Father Moore's Well in the town is preserved in a good state. Father Moore himself, who lived from 1779 until 1826, is said to have given the waters of the well wonderful curative powers. He had great powers in another way too, ensuring that candles, once lit, were never put out. Near the Church of Ireland cathedral in the town, a small road leads to the other well in Kildare town, named in honour of St Brigid, who co-founded the religious community here in the 5th century.

Clonmel

One Day

St Patrick's Well, Marlfield, Clonmel, Co. Tipperary is a very ancient holy well, with associations allegedly going back to St Patrick. In recent years the area around the well has been much modernised, so access is easy. The actual well site itself has clear running water and is still a popular place of pilgrimage. It is worth going to see, as is Clonmel itself, with its historic sites and sights.

North Midlands

One Day

Begin your day's pilgrimage at Clonmacnois, almost in the centre of Ireland. It's 21 km (13 miles) south of Athlone on the N6 and N62.

The whole site at Clonmacnois is extensive with many ruins, a cathedral and a round tower. The site was founded by St Kieran in AD 545, but nothing on the present-day site is earlier than the 9th century. The well named after him dates back to Celtic times and has three stone heads that are venerated during pilgrimages.

From Clonmacnois, drive 70 km (43 miles) northeast of Athlone, through Mullingar and Castlepollard, to Fore Abbey. This abbey is set on the northern shores of Lough Lene, just outside Castlepollard. The site dates back to the 7th century and has various features that are often described as the "Seven Wonders of Fore". One of these wonders refers to St Fechin's Well, which is in the shade of the tree that will not burn. The water from the well itself cannot be boiled, no matter how hard you try. The tree beside the well is jammed full of hundreds of coins, placed there by pilgrims who found that the waters did have a healing effect. Apart from the well itself, you will find the whole monastic site very rewarding.

From Castlepollard, drive to Longford by way of Edgesworthstown, along the R395 and N4, a distance of 35 km (21 miles). From Longford, continue through Carrick-on-Shannon, turning off at Lough Key forest park on the N4, as far as Ballyfarnan. From Longford to Ballyfarnan is 45 km (27 miles).

St Lassair's Well, near Ballyfarnan, is one of the most traditional wells in Ireland. The waters from the well have long been considered to have curative powers for anyone with back trouble. The testimony can be seen in the tree on the site, which is completely surrounded by coins, rosaries, pins and holy medals.

Sligo and Donegal

One Day

Some of Ireland's main holy wells can be visited in counties Sligo and Donegal.

Tobernalt Holy Well, Co. Sligo is really an outdoor church, near the western end of Lough Gill, about 8 km (5 miles) south-east of Sligo. The setting is wonderfully peaceful, with the waters from the well flowing into Lough Gill. The well itself is very ancient, pre-dating the arrival of Christianity in Ireland in the 5th century. The ritual and revelry of Tobernalt were embedded in Celtic culture for a thousand years before St Patrick, who is believed to have baptised the first Christians here. The well is traditionally connected with the healing of back and head pains.

One story told within the last few years testifies to its powers. A building worker on a site in Dublin suffered an accident when a reinforced rod went into one of his eyes. The surgeons did not believe they had any chance of saving the eye. A friend from Sligo visited the man in hospital and suggested trying water from Tobernalt Well. The man put some of the water in his eye and within days the eye was completely healed, without any surgery or medical intervention.

The pagan Celtic tradition of people unburdening their ills and offering petitions by leaving rags and strips torn from their clothing is still practised today. What was the Lughanasa Festival in Celtic times is now Garland Sunday, which takes place at the well on the last Sunday of July. This tradition is not unique to Tobernalt Well; many other wells in Ireland celebrate Garland Sunday on the same date. Besides the actual well, set close to the cliff face, you can see the penal cross, the Mass rock and the Lourdes grotto, for Tobernalt is still very much a place of pilgrimage.

From Tobernalt, drive 40 km (24 miles) through Sligo and Bundoran to Ballyshannon in south Donegal. On the seashore here, where the River Erne enters Donegal Bay, St Patrick's Well is a keyhole-shaped sea-water well. The flow of water is strong and clear, refreshed by the sea at high tide. The nearby iron crosses denote each ritual station. Apart from the well itself, the setting beside the seashore is magnificent.

From Ballyshannon, travel north-east to Letterkenny, 60 km (37 miles). From here, drive 10 km (6 miles) north-west on the N56 as far as Kilmacrennan.

The Doon Well here is in a very historic spot. On the hill nearby, the old chieftains of Tír Chonaill, the O'Donnells, were inaugurated for many centuries. The last inauguration took place here in 1603. The well is said to have many curative properties, and pieces of cloth that have touched the place of pain are tied to the bush beside the well for a cure to be effected. The hazel tree that stands beside the well is also venerated.

The whole site became a place of pilgrimage in the 18th century.

Struel Wells, Co. Down

One Day

These are very ancient healing wells, just 2 km (1.2 miles) east of Downpatrick, Co. Down, off the B1 road. One of the wells was used traditionally for eye bathing, while the other was used for drinking. The wells are situated beside separate bath houses for men and women, through which the water still flows. The setting, in a secluded rocky valley, is very peaceful. The ancient site is associated with St Patrick, but the present buildings only date from after 1600. Access can be made at any time.

TRAIL 15

Granuaile, The Pirate Queen

This is a three-day trail.

Granuaile (Grace O'Malley), the pirate queen of the western seas, was a remarkable adventurer, who controlled the seas off the West of Ireland in the 16th century and led a life of great daring. The daughter of Owen O'Malley, the Chief of the Western Islands, she was born about 1530 and her early childhood was spent in the O'Malley family home near Murrisk on the road from Westport to Louisburgh, and on Clare Island. When her father died, she made herself the ruler of the area around Clew Bay. She died in 1603.

CLARE ISLAND

ONE DAY

Begin the tour with a trip to Clare Island; boats leave at regular intervals from Roonagh Quay, 5 km (3 miles) west of Louisburgh. The crossing is also about 5 km (3 miles) and is best undertaken in calm summer weather.

On the island, you can visit the castle by the quay where Granuaile lived, which has had many subsequent uses, including a coastguard station and police barracks. It's considered likely that she was buried in the Carmelite friary on the island, which was built by the O'Malleys in 1224, although the present-day ruins date from a later period. Clare Island was her stronghold and walking around the small island, easily done in a few hours, will give a good sense of her seaborne heritage.

Westport House and Grounds, Co. Mayo

O'Malleys Ferries, *by Roonagh Quay; tel (098) 25045; fax (098) 26976.*
Captain Chris O'Grady, *"Pirate Queen", tel (098) 66288*

Westport

Two Days

Begin your mainland tour of places with Grace O'Malley connections at Westport House just on the outskirts of Westport. The present owner of Westport House, Lord Altamont, is the 13th great-grandson of Grace O'Malley and the house has some fine portraits showing the family connection. The house itself is one of the finest mansions in the West of Ireland, begun in 1730, with the west wing added some 50 years later. It replaces an earlier house, built in the 17th century on the site of an O'Malley castle. Besides the portraits in the magnificent main house, the grounds have many leisure attractions, including a zoo.

Westport House and Grounds, *near Westport, Co. Mayo; tel (098) 27766/25430* (open daily, June–Sept).

From Westport, take the N59 road north and then west, in the direction of Achill Island, which is 40 km (25 miles) distant, along a route that is strikingly scenic, with views over Clew Bay and its alleged 365 islands, one for every day of the year.

Three locations along this route have close associations with Grace O'Malley. Just 3 km (2 miles) beyond Newport, see the ruins of the 15th-century Burrishoole Abbey, a Dominican foundation. Some legends claim that Burrishoole and not Clare Island Abbey is the last resting place of Grace O'Malley, but the final mystery of where she is buried will probably never be solved.

In her second marriage, to MacWilliam Oughter, she lived in nearby Carrigahooley Castle. The alliance was to last a year, after which it could be terminated by either party saying "I dismiss you." She spent the year filling all the MacWilliam castles with her own supporters and at the end of the year, as MacWilliam Oughter entered the castle, Grace dismissed him for ever with the words: "I dismiss you."

She had lived in Rockfleet Castle for much of her life. It's further along the road to Achill, on an inlet of Clew Bay near Mulrany. The four-storey building is in good condition and can be visited. It's a stark building with no exterior fortification, but here, according to Anne Chambers, the contemporary expert on Grace O'Malley, if you explore this castle you will get a good feeling for the life and times of Grace O'Malley. During the summer, the castle is usually open to visitors.

Finally, on this leg of the journey, cross to Achill Island and drive to its most southerly point. Turn off the main road at Achill Sound and follow narrow badly metalled roads as far as Kildavnet Castle. It's 7 km (4 miles) south of Achill Sound. This castle was another O'Malley stronghold, but today it's in ruins, picturesquely set near the coast.

Return to Westport and take the R335 road in the direction of Louisburgh. On the southside of Clew Bay, 7 km (4 miles) from Westport, stop off at Murrisk Abbey, which was built by the ubiquitous O'Malleys in 1457. The monastery was suppressed in 1574, although Grace O'Malley's son, Theobald, made a chalice for it in 1635. Although the abbey is in ruins much remains to be seen, including an outstanding east window and one of the west doors. The setting itself is magnificent, with the 763 metre (2,503 ft) Croagh Patrick at its back and Clew Bay in front.

The nearby village of Louisburgh, 20 km (12 miles) from Westport, is not much more than the crossroads at its centre. It dates back to the 18th century, when it was laid out as a model town by the 1st Marquess of Sligo. His uncle Henry had fought against the French at the Battle of Louisburgh in Canada and that's where the name comes from. The old Church of Ireland, just off the central crossroads, had a Grace O'Malley Heritage Centre, but at the time of writing this was closed to the public. Future plans for the centre are unclear.

Two other West of Ireland locations have close connections with Grace O'Malley. After her first marriage to Donal O'Flaherty about 1546 they lived in Bunowen Castle, which is 6 km (4 miles) south-east of Slyne Head, beyond Clifden, Co. Galway, but little trace of this remains. She also owned the old fort on Inishbofin island, off the Galway coast.

For further information on Grace O'Malley, read Anne Chambers' books on the subject and contact: **Tourist Information Office**, *Westport, Co. Mayo; tel (098) 25711; fax (098) 26709* (open all year).

TRAIL 16

Lost Villages

This trail takes four days.

Scattered throughout Ireland, remnants of lost villages recall the famine era of the late 1840s, when many settlements were simply abandoned. Their inhabitants either emigrated or died. In a few instances, the foundations of their villages can still be seen, tracing eerie patterns of long-vanished village life. In one or two other cases, villages were built to house workers for long-gone industries and these remains can still be seen today. In the case of the industrial model villages, often the houses are still in good condition, perfectly habitable.

WESTMEATH

ONE DAY

One of these lost famine villages is at Carn, 16 km (10 miles) south-east of Mullingar. Take the R390 west of Mullingar to the village of Killare, then turn south on the minor road to Carn.

There, on the summit of the hill, looking over to the nearby hill of Uisneach, are the foundations of a famine village that was originally built in the early 19th century. In some cases, more than the foundations of houses have been left intact and the ruins of 16 small cottages can be seen. Most are very simple two-room buildings, which had a kitchen and a sleeping area, while several are more elaborate, once inhabited by people a little further up the social scale than labourers. Most cottages of this period were built with mud or stone walls and had thatched roofs, so they haven't survived, but the cottages at Carn were stone built and have survived to a greater degree. So well preserved is the little settlement that even the outlines of the cottage gardens can be made out. Standing in the midst of these ruins, with the elevated situation giving good views of the locality, it's easy to imagine what life was like nearly two hundred years ago.

A decade before the famine struck, a Poor Law Commission report said that only 60 per cent of the labourers and cottiers in the area had constant work and when they were not working, lived on a meagre diet of potatoes and salt. Charles Kelly, who was a pre-famine Justice of the Peace in the parish of Conroy, where Carn is situated, described the clothing of the 100 labourers who lived in the parish as being "very middling, generally frieze". When the potato crop was devastated during the famine, families in Carn, as well as those in countless other parts of the west and south, had no food for their survival. The famine village of Carn remains today as a bleak testament to the suffering of that long-distant era.

ACHILL ISLAND

ONE DAY

On Achill Island, on the west coast of Co. Mayo, there's an even more spectacularly-set deserted village, Slievemore. It's on the slopes of Slievemore mountain (671 metres/2,023 ft). The mountain is strange and brooding, a mass of quartzite rock, with occasional shining masses of mica. On the eastern slopes of this mountain, between the villages of Keel and Dugort, there are well-preserved remains of a deserted village. In the 10 to 15 years before the famine, Achill started to be developed, not always in harmonious ways. A small Protestant settlement was established on the island and attempts were made to convert the population. On a happier note, the first hotel on the island was built in 1835, attracting the very first tourists to Achill. Tourism has been the mainstay of the island economy ever since.

In the early 19th century, with tourism only starting, the economy on Achill was primitive, entirely dependent on subsistence farming. Any developed villages, such as Keel, had little more than an unpaved mud-covered street, a few desolate cabins and some more elaborate two-storey stone-built houses.

Yet despite these conditions of great poverty, Achill Island managed to support around 8,000 people, or four times the present permanent population. One of the settlements on the island that was well populated before the famine was

Slievemore. The famine destroyed the village, but many of the remains of the houses can still be seen now, together with remains of a more ancient lineage, including dolmens, stone circles and prehistoric tumuli.

DUBLIN

ONE DAY

While settlements like Carn and Slievemore were agricultural and consequently destroyed by the effects of the famine, another type of settlement began to be created in the early 19th century. Industry started to be developed in Ireland. A whole village grew up around the new railway works in Inchicore, Dublin, which were opened in 1846. Many of those railway houses can still be seen today in the Ranch district of Inchicore.

Trams were another form of public transport developed in the late 19th century and in certain areas of Dublin, such as Donnybrook and Sandymount, you can see the old tramway cottages built close to the tram depots. These brick cottages, usually one storey, were built to last and they are just as solid today, often much refurbished.

In Gilford Terrace in the Sandymount district of Dublin, just off Gilford Road and close to the Martello tower, there are two rows of old tramway cottages, still lived in today. The old tram depot beside them is now part of an advertising agency.

CLONMEL AND WATERFORD

ONE DAY

One of the most spectacular industrial housing projects from early 19th-century Ireland was located in Clonmel, Co. Tipperary. Just west of the town, beyond Westgate and just off Marlfield Road, is the old village of Marlfield. It's not quite a deserted village, because the houses are still inhabited, but it's a most striking collection of estate houses.

They are very reminiscent of an old English village and they were built for the workers at the long-vanished

Marlfield whiskey distillery. The name "Marlfield" came originally from the marl, a type of limestone found in this area that was used for brick making. There is also a lake, which was an artificial creation, the work of Stephen Moore, who in 1769 created the six-hectare lake from a swamp. Now designated as a wildfowl conservancy area, it has an enormous stock of wildfowl and is a recognised breeding ground for several species of birds.

(Similar workers' houses can be seen at Sion Mills in Co. Tyrone, on the main road from Omagh to Strabane. The Herdman family built large linen mills in the village – the same textile manufacturers are there to this day – and in the early 19th century, they built many cottages for the millworkers. They were built to last and survive, often much refurbished.)

From Clonmel, travel 50 km (31 miles) south-east along the N24 to Waterford city, then to Passage East. Follow the signs from Waterford for the Passage East car ferry. Three km (2 miles) south of Passage East stands Geneva Barracks.

This was once a new town, built in 1793 to house refugee Swiss watchmakers. They stayed briefly, then abandoned the settlement that had been built for them. In the immediate aftermath of the 1798 Rebellion, the buildings were used to house many captured rebels. Geneva Barracks became notorious for the many atrocities committed within their walls. Subsequently, the barracks were abandoned permanently and fell into ruin. Today, the very substantial outward walls remain largely intact. Each of the walls is 400 metres long, but of the rest of the settlement nothing is to be seen. The site has long since reverted to its original fields.

TRAIL 17

Railways

With some 30 sites all over Ireland devoted to railway heritage, including some with working sections of track, enthusiasts will have a field day. Two trails are suggested: a five-day tour starting in Northern Ireland and concluding in Co. Leitrim, and a four-day tour taking in sites in Southern Ireland.

DOWNPATRICK

ONE DAY

Start this trail at the Railway Museum in Downpatrick, where considerable work has already been done on preserving the atmosphere of the old Belfast and County Down Railway. The old station building, which was originally part of the town's old gasworks, was dismantled and rebuilt, winning a major railway heritage award in the process. Inside the building, there's a collection of photographs of the old railway. The signal cabin too was dismantled and restored; originally, it was at King's Bog Junction, near Ballyclare, Co. Antrim. In the sidings stand two locomotives originally built for industrial use in the south, one for Guinness, the other for the Irish Sugar Company.

Some diesel engines that once belonged to CIÉ are now themselves museum pieces and are on display. The museum also has a useful selection of restored carriages, including the Royal Saloon, built for the Belfast and County Down Railway in 1897, and a superb coach from the old Great Southern and Western Railway. You can look around the workshops and see carriages and locomotives being restored, while there are trips on the 5 ft 3 in. gauge track from the station. At present, the trains are run as far as King Magnus's Halt, a round trip of about 30 minutes.

Plans are under way to extend the working track to Ballydugan, on the Newcastle side of Downpatrick, and to Inch Abbey station on the Belfast side. You can even take a six-hour footplate experience course at the controls of a steam train.

Downpatrick Railway Society, *The Railway Station, Market Street, Downpatrick, Co. Down; tel (02844) 615779.*

Giant's Causeway & Bushmills Railway line

GIANT'S CAUSEWAY

ONE DAY

Giant's Causeway & Bushmills Railway opened in 2000, the latest addition to the North's railway heritage. It runs from Bushmills to the Giant's Causeway on the north coast and includes track and engine from the old narrow gauge railway at Shane's Castle, Co. Antrim. It's been a long time, nearly 60 years, since the old hydro-electric tram ran from Portrush to the Giant's Causeway, so this new railway will re-create much of that old magic. The new track runs along a modern bridge across the River Bush. All along the track views of the coastline add to the splendours of the trip.

Giant's Causeway & Bushmills Railway, *Co. Antrim; tel (02820) 741157.*

Traditional new locomotive buildings for the Giant's Causeway & Bushmills Railway

CULTRA

ONE DAY

The Ulster Folk & Transport Museum, just outside Holywood, Co. Down, has a highly impressive Irish Railway Collection. The highlight of this collection is the "Maeve", the great steam leviathan built at the Inchicore Railway Works in Dublin in 1939 and used primarily on the Dublin–Cork route. It continued as a working locomotive until 1958 and achieved a maximum speed of 154 kph (96 mph). The collection has many other examples of old steam locomotives and carriages from all over Ireland.

Ulster Folk & Transport Museum, *Cultra, Co. Down; tel (02890) 428428/421444* (open daily, all year).

FOYLE VALLEY

ONE DAY

Over in Derry, the Foyle Valley Railway Centre, beside the River Foyle and Craigavon Bridge, has an amazing collection of old engines and carriages, realistically restored. They include equipment from the old narrow gauge County Donegal Railway and the Londonderry and Lough Swilly Railway Company. All the exhibits are housed in an old railway station, so the atmosphere is very authentic. Working train trips operate on the track beside the river; the track extends for 9 km (6 miles) beside the River Foyle. Two diesel railcars are used, one from 1932, the other from 1940. There are ambitious plans to extend into Co. Donegal, re-creating in part the old County Donegal Railway system.

Foyle Valley Railway Centre, *Derry; tel (02871) 265234 (open all year, Tues–Sat).*

DONEGAL AND LEITRIM

ONE DAY

From Derry, travel into west Donegal, to see the working stretch of line at Fintown, near Glenties, where 2 miles of track has been restored. Diesel engines haul the carriages.

St Conal's Museum in Glenties itself has a good collection of artefacts, including photographs and posters, from the old County Donegal Railway. The railway museum in Donegal Town similarly preserves many aspects of the old Donegal system.

County Donegal Railway, *tel (075) 46280.*
St Conal's Museum, Glenties, *Co. Donegal; tel (075) 51265* (open May–Sept, Mon–Sat, or by arrangement).
County Donegal Railway Museum, *Donegal; tel (073) 22655* (open daily).

From Donegal, move on to the railway museum at Dromod, Co. Leitrim. The old station here, once part of the narrow gauge Cavan and Leitrim Railway, which opened in 1887 and closed in 1958, has a collection of old photographs. The ticket office and waiting room have been restored, while in the adjacent carriage shed stand several restored carriages. The engine shed and water tower have also been restored. Working steam train trips operate on about half a mile of track, but much more ambitious plans are under way to reinstate the track for an 8 km (5 miles) stretch to Mohill, where the station is being restored.

Cavan and Leitrim Railway Museum, *Dromod, Co. Leitrim; tel (078) 38599.*

Listowel

One Day

Start this four-day trail in Munster, where two major railway projects are well under way. In Listowel, Co. Kerry, work is progressing to restore the Lartigue railway, which was a unique monorail system that operated between 1886 and 1924. The single track was about one metre off the ground and the carriages were on both sides of the track, so they had to be carefully balanced before the train set off on the 9-mile journey from Listowel to Ballybunion.

In the first part of the plan, a short section of track is being rebuilt in Listowel, 500 metres long. A Lartigue locomotive is being re-created along with two carriages, and these will be used for working trips. It's hoped that this section of track will be ready in 2001. The second section of the project will be the museum.

Lartigue Railway, *Listowel, Co. Kerry; details from Jimmy Deenihan, Committee Chairman, tel (068) 40235/40154.*

ENNIS

ONE DAY

From 1893 the West Clare Railway, which ran from Ennis, Co. Clare, to the west coast of the county, provided transport for local people and inspiration for Percy French, the songwriter, with his song "Are you right there, Michael, are you right?" The line closed down in 1961, at a time of great railway rationalisation, but was always sorely missed.

At Moyasta Junction, near Ennis, 5 km (3 miles) of track have been relaid and the old engine that once stood at Ennis railway station is now restored and back in action. Regular train trips are organised during the summer and plans are underway to restore the line.

West Clare Railway, *tel (065) 9051284.*

WATERFORD

ONE DAY

The 22-mile section of the Waterford–Dungarvan line has long been closed, but a 5-mile stretch starting at Ferrybank in Waterford is in the process of being restored and should be ready for 2001. A diesel locomotive and two carriages will run tours on this track section.

Waterford & Suir Valley Railway, *details from Paul Cassidy, tel (051) 858215.*

MULLINGAR

ONE DAY

The most exciting railway and transport plans are scheduled for Mullingar, Co. Westmeath, where plans are under way for a National Transport Museum. This will include the restoration of the disused part of Mullingar railway station, the restoration of other old buildings, such as the engine shed and water tower, and working steam train trips to Athlone. It's due to start becoming operational in 2002.

National Transport Museum, *Mullingar, Co. Westmeath; details from Mullingar Tourist Information Office, tel (044) 48650.*

Useful reading: Bord Fáilte and the Northern Ireland Tourist Board publish an all-Ireland information guide to steam trains and railway centres throughout Ireland.

TRAIL 18

Seán Ó Riada

Seán Ó Riada (1931–1971) was one of Ireland's greatest musical geniuses, an outstanding performer of Irish traditional music and an even more renowned and original composer. To follow the places most closely connected with him means a one-day tour in counties Cork and Limerick and a one-day tour in Dublin.

CORK AND LIMERICK

ONE DAY

Seán Ó Riada was born in Cork, but brought up in Co. Limerick. His father was a Garda sergeant and his mother was a concertina and melodeon player. Both parents came from a farming background and were very culturally aware. Seán lived first of all in Adare, where he attended the Christian Brothers School from the age of 4; Brother Long at the school laid the foundations for Seán's lifelong love of Irish.

From Adare, travel 25 km (15 miles) via Croom on the N20 and R516 to the small village of Bruff. When Seán Ó Riada's father was transferred here, the family spent several more years living in this village. Bruff doesn't have the picturesque qualities of Adare, with thatched cottages lining the Main Street, but it's an attractive village nevertheless. From Bruff, the young Seán made the short journey (20 km/12 miles) into Limerick city. There, from the age of 7, he studied violin with Granville Metcalfe. When he was 10, he joined the Limerick Club, noted for its music making.

From 1943 until 1947, Seán was at boarding school, Farranferris Seminary School in Co. Cork. When he completed his studies there, being too young to go to university he went to St Munchin's College in Limerick. In 1948, he went to University College, Cork on a scholarship, where he studied arts, along with music, Greek, Latin and Irish, under the renowned Professor Aloys Fleischmann. A stroll around the central campus of University College, Cork, and a visit to its music department, will be rewarding. As soon as Seán graduated from UCC, he joined Radio Éireann in Dublin as assistant director of music. His life in Dublin is covered in that section. That year, 1953, was equally momentous in another way for Seán – he married Ruth Coghlan, with whom he had seven children.

One of those children, Peadar, lives in the same area where his father spent the latter part of his life. Seán moved to An Draighean, Cúil Aodha (Coolea), a small village 20 km (12 miles) west of Macroom. Coolea and nearby Ballyvourney are two small rural and largely unspoiled villages in north-west Cork. In the late 1960s, Seán became ill and in 1971 he spent some time in the Bon Secours Hospital, Cork, and then at King's College Hospital, London, where he died in October 1971.

Seán Ó Riada is buried in St Gobnait's graveyard at Ballyvourney. Nearby is buried another artistic genius who died young, the Waterford-born poet and writer, Seán Dunne, who worked for many years for the Cork Examiner and who died in August 1995, aged 38.

DUBLIN

ONE DAY

Most of Seán Ó Riada's career was in Dublin. You can see the exterior of the GPO in O'Connell Street; once the upper floors of the GPO housed the studios of Radio Éireann and it was here that Seán began the first job of his career, as assistant music director. He left Radio Éireann in 1955 and went to Paris for a year, where he worked for ORTF, the French State broadcasting organisation, on its radio service. When he returned home to Ireland, he said that he would rather be breaking stones in Ireland than living as the richest man in Europe.

When he returned to Dublin, he did much arranging work for the Radio Éireann Singers and the Radio Éireann Light Orchestra and he was also appointed musical director for the Abbey Theatre. The theatre is only 300 metres from the GPO and you may wish to look around the foyer to see

mementoes of the many renowned artistic figures who worked for the Abbey. A substantial programme of improvements is under way at the Abbey.

In many ways, 1959 was a memorable year for Seán Ó Riada and his family. They went on holiday that summer to Corca Dhuibhne, the Co. Kerry Gaeltacht, which was Seán's first contact with the Gaeltacht, an immense culturally rewarding experience that had a profound impact for the rest of his life.

It saw the first appearance of the group that evolved from the various musicians surrounding Seán Ó Riada. The group, known as Ceoltóirí Chualann, made their first performance at the Shelbourne Hotel, Dublin, in the autumn of 1959, part of the Dublin Theatre Festival. The group had a big following in the 1960s, with their extremely original renditions of Irish traditional music. Their final performance was in Cork City Hall in 1969. One of the most notable songs sung by Seán Ó Sé, the legendary Cork schoolmaster, with the group was "An Poc ar Buile".

When you are making the pilgrimage around the Ó Riada sites, you may want to play some of his music, or music by Ceoltóirí Chualann on your Walkman. It's incredibly lively and fresh, highly original even after all these years.

In the Horse Shoe Bar in the Shelbourne, you could raise a toast to Seán Ó Riada and his genius. You could do the same in a number of pubs that he and his group frequented, including McDaids and Nearys, just off the top of Grafton Street. The Brazen Head in Lower Bridge Street claims to be Dublin's oldest pub – a pub has been on this site since the 12th century. Seán and his musical friends, including Garech de Brún, often had sessions in the Brazen Head. One of the songs that Seán liked to sing there was "The Enniskillen Dragoons". At closing time, the potboy, called Alec, closed the gates to the pub so that the guests could not get out and the guards could not get in.

Another favourite pub of Seán's was Hartigan's in Lower Leeson Street, close to where Garech de Brún then lived in Quinn's Lane. His flat there often saw lively, impromptu music sessions taking place.

In Hartigan's, one of Seán Ó Riada's favourite tipples was The Wedge – one or more Irish whiskies, wedged between a pint of stout. Other noted places closely associated with Seán Ó Riada, including the original Bailey's pub in Duke Street and Jammets Restaurant in Nassau Street, no longer exist.

In many ways, Seán had childlike impulses. In the days when he was freelancing, working for RTÉ and The Irish Times, as soon as he got a cheque he was quite likely to take friends to lunch and enjoy the proceeds at the Red Bank, another noted Dublin restaurant that once stood in D'Olier Street, opposite The Irish Times.

When he and his family were living in Galloping Green, Stillorgan, he had a second-hand Jaguar car for a while. It's worth making the trip out to Galloping Green, which is on the main N11 9 km (6 miles) south of the city centre. Going out of town, on the left-hand side, Byrne's pub is one of the last untouched, country-style pubs left in the Dublin area. Thankfully, it hasn't been "improved" to date and you can savour Seán Ó Riada's memory in its wood-panelled quietude. The modest two-storey house dating back to Victorian times, that stands 50 metres on the cityward side of the pub, was the Ó Riada house, where impromptu céili sessions were often held.

His musical talent was incredible; not only was he inspired by the great legacy of Irish traditional music, including O'Carolan, but he derived his influences from Arabic and Indian music which he considered to have close links with Irish music. His time in Dublin was very productive, with such scores as that for the Mise Éire film made by George Morrison in 1960, a stunning compilation of newsreel material from the War of Independence, and the score for the An Tine Bheo film (same director), made for the 50th anniversary of the Easter Rising, in 1966. He wrote the music for the 1961 film version of Playboy of the Western World, and two years later wrote the music for John Ford's film about Sean O'Casey, Young Cassidy. During his time in Coolea, just 15 km (9 miles) from where his very musical mother was born, in Kilnamartyra, he formed the local choir and wrote more than seven hundred arrangements of songs and dances for traditional groups. In 1968, he wrote a commissioned piece for RTÉ on the Battle of Aughrim.

His very last recorded piece, for harpsichord, "Ó Riada's Farewell", was published just before he died. Seán Ó Riada made an extraordinary contribution to Irish music in the 20th century, a wholly original reworking of many traditional pieces.

For further information on his life and work: **Irish Traditional Music Archive**, *63 Merrion Square, Dublin 2; tel (01) 661 9699; fax (01) 662 4585; website www.itma.ie* (open Mon–Fri l0am–lpm, 2pm–5pm).

To see performances of his work on video: visit **Ceol, the traditional Irish music museum**, *Smithfield, Dublin; tel (01) 817 3820; fax (01) 817 3821; email info@ceol.ie; website www.ceol.ie* (buses from Middle Abbey Street and Aston Quay, as far as Merchant's Quay; then cross the river to Smithfield).

TRAIL 19

Industrial Archaeology

This trail would take about two weeks.

Many locations around Ireland offer compelling insights into Ireland's industrial past. The number of locations is comparatively limited, with a certain dependence on old brewing, distilling and mining operations, the result of Ireland's late emergence as an industrial country. Apart from Belfast, the traditional engineering environment of the 19th century simply did not develop in Ireland as it did in France, Germany, the UK or US. The real industrial development in Ireland has only come in the past twenty years and since so much of it is electronically related, computer hardware and software, it's too new to have any heritage.

DUBLIN AND THE EAST COAST

THREE DAYS

Three very profitable days can be spent exploring locations in Dublin and along the east coast of Ireland.

In Dublin, Guinness has carried out a major redevelopment of its visitor centre, which used to be in the Hopstore, just off Thomas Street. The premises have now been taken over by the European multimedia laboratories of the Massachussets Institute of Technology. Guinness has spent IR£30 million converting a 1904 building, on the Guinness site in Dublin, into the Storehouse experience. This now houses a world-class visitor experience explaining the whole Guinness story, how the famous beverage is brewed and how it is transported around the world.

A fascinating addition is the Guinness advertising archives, with the whole history of Guinness advertising, including its memorable Gilroy cartoons done in the 1930s. Visitors can access this archive, then when they have completed their tour, beginning in the giant pint-glass atrium, they can go to the rooftop bar for a sample of the black stuff and one of the best rooftop views in the city.

The Guinness Storehouse, *Dublin; tel (01) 408 4800; fax (01) 408 4965; website: www.guinness.com* (open daily all year).

From Guinness, travel 750 metres across the River Liffey to the Old Jameson Distillery in Bow Street. This is a marvellous reconstruction of the distilling experience that began in this area of Dublin over two centuries ago. The original Jameson distillery was set up here in 1780. The centre has much of the old equipment, including mash tuns and wooden fermentation vessels and the original copper stills. The maturing warehouse has been re-created and there's also a working bottling line. It's an excellent reconstruction, spirited and full of atmosphere. The centre has a fine audio-visual presentation that tells the whole history of Irish whiskey. The tour also includes tastings, restaurant, bar and shopping facilities, so for visitors it's a very complete experience.

Old Jameson Distillery, *Bow Street, Dublin; tel (01) 807 2355; fax (01) 807 2369* (open daily except Christmas Day and Good Friday, with tours run regularly throughout the day, 9.30am–5pm. Closes at 6pm).

While Guinness dates back to the mid 1750s and the distilling tradition that culminated in Irish Distillers began just 30 years later, the oldest firm in Dublin, Rathborne's candle factory on the East Wall Road, founded in 1488, doesn't have a heritage centre but does have a book on its history.

The other industrial museum in Dublin that's well worth a visit is the National Print Museum in the former Beggar's Bush Barracks at the foot of Haddington Road, on the city's southside.

The old military chapel has been tastefully converted into a museum on two levels, with fine examples of old printing equipment, including presses, Linotype machines that once set type in hot metal (before computers took over) and binding equipment. The museum has lots of other memorabilia, including photographs and old newspapers, together with video presentations that tell the story of old-style printing. Within the past 20 years, hot metal and letterpress printing has disappeared totally, so the museum performs a useful preservation function. It also has a coffee shop, where you can reminisce over a cup or two.

Rathborne's candle factory, *East Wall Road, Dublin; tel (01) 874 3515; website www.rathborne.ie.*
National Print Museum, *Haddington Road, Dublin; tel (01) 660 3770* (open daily, all year).

It's worth travelling 75 km (50 miles) north of Dublin to the County Louth Museum in the centre of Dundalk. On the way there, stop off at Skerries, 20 km (12 miles) north of Dublin. The Skerries Mill is a reconstruction of four- and five-sail windmills, complete with demonstrations of corn grinding.

Going on to Dundalk, the county museum is a recent creation, made when an 18th-century warehouse was turned into a museum focusing strongly on Dundalk's industrial traditions. The town had many traditional specialities, including railway engineering, brewing and shoe making. All are chronicled in imaginative fashion.

The centre even has a bubble car made by Henkel in the town in 1960. Not only are the exhibits well presented, but multimedia technology is used to good effect. The centre also has extensive archives, for instance, on the Dundalk Democrat, one of the two newspapers in the town. It was the last newspaper in Ireland to change its front page from the old format of all small advertisements, which only happened in 2000.

The trip to Dundalk and its museum would make an excellent one-day visit in its own right.

Skerries Mill, *Skerries, Co. Dublin; tel (01) 849 5208* (open all year, daily).
County Louth Museum, *Dundalk, Co. Louth; tel (042) 9327056/7; email dlkmuseum@eircom.net* (open May–Sept, Mon–Sat l0.30am–5.30pm, Sun and bank holidays 2pm–6pm; Oct–April, Tues–Sat l0.30am–5.30pm, Sun 2pm–6pm).

If you go to Straffan, 20 km (15 miles) west of Dublin (turn off the N7 at Kill), the steam museum has lots of old steam engines, mostly from industrial locations, some in working order. They were once used to power processes in such locations as the Jameson Distillery in Dublin, the Midleton Distillery in Co. Cork and Smithwicks Brewery in Kilkenny. The centre also includes models and has a cafe.

Straffan Steam Museum, *Straffan, Co. Kildare; tel (01) 627 3155* (open daily April–Sept, or by arrangement).

To the south of Dublin, the first suggested call is to the old lead mines at Ballycorus, which is approached from the main N11, turning off at the Silver Tassie pub in Loughlinstown. Go up Cherrywood Road, Bride's Glen and Ballycorus Road, as far as Sutton Lane. From the N11, the distance is 3 km (2 miles). From Sutton Lane, you can drive to the top of Mill Hill Lane, but for the rest of the distance you must climb on foot. The old mining operations here were busy during the 19th century, but all that's left now is the old mine chimney. It's a landmark for miles around and is also a fine viewpoint. However, since this was once an active lead-mining operation, take care as you walk around the area.

Travel further south into Co. Wicklow, for another 70 km (43 miles), travelling through Rathdrum, to Avoca, otherwise known as the setting for *Ballykissangel*. Plans are under way to develop the abandoned mining area here where mining only ceased in the 1950s. All the old mine buildings will be preserved, with the old office being the focal point for the walkways that are planned around the area – it will contain a museum, with plenty of mining memorabilia. Many of the old buildings, including the mine chimney, are extant. The planned memorial park will feature a display of old and modern mining equipment. All this development is likely to take two to three years to complete; in the meantime, you can walk around the site, but do take great care. Further details from the Wicklow town tourism office,

The last site in Co. Wicklow is in the heart of Arklow, 12 km (8 miles) south-east of Avoca. Arklow, a coastal industrial town, isn't the most prepossessing place and it's had a long history of economic under-performance and unemployment, which now seems to be lifting. But two of its great traditions, shipbuilding and seafaring, are well documented in the maritime museum. This is a real old-fashioned museum, with no fancy multimedia or modern presentations apart from some videos, but nonetheless it's a fascinating insight into the old seafaring ways. All sorts of old maritime equipment including navigation equipment is there.

The old schooners, brigs and brigantines that once

sailed out of Arklow are honoured and so too is the present-day Arklow Shipping Company, which has the largest fleet of ships flying the Irish flag.

The museum also commemorates the fact that Arklow has the oldest RNLI (lifeboat) station in Ireland. There's even a shoe that was once worn by a female passenger on the ill-fated Lusitania, which sank off the Old Head of Kinsale in 1915.

Tourist Office, *Wicklow; tel (0404) 69117; fax (0404) 69118; email wicklowtouristoffice@eircom.net.*

Arklow Maritime Museum, *St Mary's Road, Arklow, Co. Wicklow; tel (0402) 32868* (open all year, Mon–Sat l0am–1pm, 2pm–5pm, and by arrangement).

WATERFORD AND CORK

THREE DAYS

This extensive trip begins with Waterford Crystal on the outskirts of Waterford city. Crystal glass making has been an integral part of Waterford's industrial tradition since the late 18th century. Since the late 1940s, the industry has been greatly revived. The new Waterford Crystal Visitor Centre shows how the glass is made and how the master-blowers create fantastic shapes with the molten glass, at temperatures of 1400 degrees centigrade. The centre gives an excellent insight into the whole process and you can see an incredible display of finished products. The centre has large shopping facilities and a fine restaurant.

Waterford Crystal Visitor Centre, *Waterford; tel (051) 332500; fax (051) 332720* (open daily March–Dec; Jan–Feb, five days a week).

From Waterford city, drive 25 km (15 miles) south-east, through the resort town of Tramore, to the south coast of Co. Waterford.

Around the Bunmahon area, there are still extensive remains of the old copper mining industry that flourished here in the 19th century. Some of the old buildings still remain, but many of the old mine shafts have never been filled in and are still very dangerous for the visitor walking the territory. As yet, no efforts have been made to create heritage centres or use other means of telling the old Waterford mining story – it's all down to what you will see on the ground along the coastline here.

For details on the area's mining history: *Des Cowman of the Bunmahon Heritage Society and the Mining Heritage Society of Ireland; tel (051) 396157.*

Some of the villages along this coast, by way of visual compensation, are very attractive, the likes of Annestown and Stradbally. Continue 75 km (46 miles) west along the N25, through Dungarvan and Youghal, as far as Midleton.

The Old Jameson Distillery Heritage Centre is one of the best industrial heritage sites in Munster. For over 150 years, whiskey was distilled here; production was transferred to the state-of-the-art plant nearby in the late 1970s. All the old distillation equipment is preserved, along with the giant waterwheels. You can see the world's largest pot still and tour around the old buildings, while there are lots of old artefacts, working models and audio-visual presentations, as well as a shop and restaurant.

Old Midleton Distillery, *Midleton, Co. Cork; tel (021) 4613594; fax (021) 4613642* (open all year, daily).

From Midleton, drive the 20 km (12 miles) into Cork city. In Cork itself, few industrial traditions have been preserved in museum format, although the Cork Heritage Park at Blackrock does have some details of Cork industries, such as boatbuilding.

In Shandon, on Cork's northside and just across the road from the famous Shandon Bells, the Cork Butter Museum recalls the great days of butter trading. During the 19th century and into the early years of the 20th century, butter was brought from all over Cork and Kerry into the port of Cork for exporting all over the world, the start of Ireland's great tradition of dairy exports.

On the western side of Cork city, at Sunday's Well, in the rather incongruous setting of the former women's jail, now restored as a museum, is the RTÉ broadcasting museum. It was sited here because in the mid 1920s, Radio Éireann, the predecessor of RTÉ, began its services in Cork from studios rigged

up in the old jail. The museum tells the story of Irish radio, including its personalities.

Cork Heritage Park, *Bessboro, Blackrock, Cork; tel (021) 4358854* (open all year, daily).

Cork Butter Museum, *Shandon, Cork; tel (021) 4300600* (open all year, daily).

Cork City Gaol, *Convent Avenue, Sunday's Well, Cork; tel (021) 4305022* (open all year, daily).

Old Midleton Distillery, Midleton, Co. Cork

At Ballincollig, 8 km (5 miles) west of Cork city, on the N22 to Killarney, the old Gunpowder Mills have been restored. Gunpowder was made here for over a century, from 1794 to 1903, for military, mine and railway construction use. The mills, set beside the River Lee, can be explored on a guided tour that includes a reconstruction of the wooden mill where the gunpowder was mixed. The tour includes an audio-visual presentation. **Ballincollig Gunpowder Mills**, *Ballincollig, Co. Cork; tel (021) 4874430* (open April–Sept, Sun–Fri; Oct–March, by arrangement).

The final visit in Cork is right over in the west of the county, at Allihies on the Beara peninsula, which is 150 km (93 miles) west of Cork. Travel through Bandon, Clonakilty, Skibbereen, Bantry, Glengarriff and Castletownbere. It's a long trek, but well worth the journey. The Beara peninsula is one of the most remote and unspoiled places in Ireland. At the far west of the peninsula, Allihies is the setting for what was Ireland's greatest copper mining industry in the 19th century. At its peak, the

115

mine here employed over 1,000 people and today substantial remains are still in place, including the steam engine houses with their tall chimneys and other mine-related buildings and sites.

Details from: **Beara Tourism & Development Association**, *The Square, Castletownbere, Co. Cork; tel/fax (027) 70054.*

GALWAY AND MAYO

ONE DAY

Four fascinating sites can be seen in the one day, beginning with the Foxford Woollen Mills in Foxford which were created in the late 19th century to create employment in this economically deprived area. In the heritage centre, you can see a very faithful re-creation of what working life was like in the old mills. You can also see present day craftspeople making the world-famous Foxford tweeds. The shop here has plenty of modern products from the mill for sale. Art galleries, craft centres, shop and restaurant are also included on the site.

Foxford Woollen Mills, *Foxford, Co. Mayo; tel (094) 56756; fax (094) 56794* (open all year, daily).

From Foxford, drive 70 km (43 miles) south to Tuam. This is a fine old town and part of its industrial heritage has been preserved in the Tuam Mill Museum. This documents the history of the building itself, the milling that was once done here and the miller's family. The mill itself closed down in 1964, but it has been back in working order since 1980; it's a preserved mill rather than a working mill and all the machinery is just as it was. The museum also includes details of the different types of mill used in the West of Ireland.

Tuam Mill Museum, *Tuam, Co. Galway; tel (093) 25486* (open June–Sept daily, or by arrangement).

From Tuam, drive the 60 km (37 miles) to Oughterard, via Galway, for yet another mine, but an interesting one nevertheless. The entrance is 3 km (2 miles) west of Oughterard, just off the main Galway–Clifden N59 road.

The Glengowla lead and silver mine was abandoned in l865, but it has now been reopened for visitors. It's the only mine in Ireland where you can walk through the tunnels and caverns, quite spectacular in their own right. You can also visit the heritage and visitor centre and see the paymaster's office and the blacksmith's.

From Oughterard, return the 25 km (15 miles) to Galway city, where there's a really fascinating new museum, the Old Waterworks Museum. Here, you can see the old city waterworks, including turbines and pumps.

Glengowla Visitor Centre, *near Oughterard, Co. Galway; tel (091) 552360/552021; (087) 2529850; email glen-gowlamines@eircom.net* (open March–Nov, daily; Dec–Feb, open most weekends).

Old Waterworks Museum, *Dyke Road, Terryland, Galway; tel (091) 536400* (open all year, daily).

MID-WEST

ONE DAY

In Limerick city, see the civic museum in its new location near King John's Castle. The museum has a wide range of material on Limerick social life and history, including the city's crafts and industries. Butter making and bacon curing, two of Limerick's old specialities, are well covered.

Limerick Museum, *Castle Lane, Limerick; tel (061) 319910* (open daily, all year).

From Limerick, drive 35 km (21 miles) west along the N69 as far as Foynes. The Flying Boat Museum here has excellent material on the flying boat era on the Shannon, immediately before and during the Second World War. Lots of exhibits, old equipment and a 1940s-style cinema for seeing the newsreels of the time make it a very interesting museum visit.

From Foynes, drive 40 km (24 miles), via Askeaton, Rathkeale and Adare, to the village of Croom. The old flour mills here have been dramatically restored showing working conditions for 19th-century millers and blacksmiths. An audio-visual presentation details the history of milling in the area. There are craft shops and restaurants.

Flying Boat Museum, *Foynes, Co. Limerick; tel/fax (069) 65416; email famm@tinet.ie* (open daily April–Oct, or by arrangement).

Croom Flour Mills, *Croom, Co. Limerick; tel (061) 397130; fax (061) 397199* (open daily all year).

MIDLANDS

TWO DAYS

The Midlands is one of the most productive areas of the country in terms of industrial archaeology. The best place to start is at the Peatland World Centre at Lullymore, 24 km (15 miles) north of Kildare town. The extraction of peat has been perhaps the prime industry for the midlands for more than 50 years and this museum is fascinating in telling the whole story, including living conditions for workers, the equipment used (complete with examples of old turf-cutting tools) and the flora and fauna. The early Christian heritage of Ireland is told in the adjacent centre. **Peatland World Centre**, *Lullymore, Co. Kildare; tel (045) 860133* (open March–Oct, Mon–Fri 9am–5pm, Sat–Sun 2pm–6pm; Nov–Feb, Mon–Fri 9am–5pm).

Return to Kildare town, then drive south-west for 40 km (24 miles) to Abbeyleix. Two priceless heritage examples can be inspected here. Firstly, there's Morrissey's pub and grocery shop, which hasn't been changed since 1900. You can see all the original fittings as well as many examples of early food packaging. You can round off your visit with a drink or two, perhaps a coffee. Also in Abbeyleix, the heritage centre details the history of the town's long-defunct carpet factory. It made high-grade carpets, including those for the ill-fated Titanic.
Abbeyleix Heritage Centre, *Abbeyleix, Co. Laois; tel (0502) 31653.*

Travel on to Castlecomer, once one of the centres for coal mining in Ireland. It's a distance of 25 km (15 miles) south-east, by back roads. Extensive coal deposits were mined in this area for centuries. The village itself was created, in the style of an Italian village, in 1635 by Sir Christopher Wandesforde, whose family began developing the mines at that time. The family controlled the mining here for the next three centuries and mining finally ended only about 30 years ago.

Not far from here, you can see more steam history at the steam museum in the picturesque town of Stradbally. This site also has a narrow gauge railway that is operated occasionally, especially bank holidays.

For more information on coal mining tradition, consult: **Castlecomer Library**, *Kilkenny Street, Castlecomer, Co. Kilkenny; tel (056) 40055; email comlibrary@eircom.net. Stradbally Steam Museum, Stradbally, Co. Laois; tel (0502) 25444.*

From Stradbally, turn north again, towards Tullamore, almost in the heart of the midlands. It's a distance of 40 km (25 miles), via Portlaoise and Mountmellick. In Tullamore, the Williams Distillery long featured in the town's industrial history. The Tullamore Dew brand had its origins here and the story of whiskey and Irish Mist liqueur can be traced in the heritage centre.

More distilling history can be seen at Kilbeggan, on the main road from Dublin to Mullingar. It's 10 km (6 miles) north of Tullamore. Locke's Distillery dates back to the 18th century and had a very colourful history, even by the standards of whiskey distilleries. It's the last example of a small pot still distillery in Ireland; whiskey was made here for 200 years.

The old working areas of the distillery have been well preserved, from the waterwheel through the mash tuns to the area where the coopers made the barrels. Nearly all the machinery has been restored and can be seen in working order. The new exhibition area contains a collection of artefacts relating to both Locke's and the distilling industry. The complex is run by the local community, and has a shop and cafe.

Tullamore Dew Heritage Centre, *Tullamore, Co. Offaly; tel (0506) 25015* (open all year, daily).

Locke's Distillery, *Kilbeggan, Co. Westmeath; tel/fax (0506) 32134* (open all year, daily).

Finally, in the very north of this area around Arigna in Co. Roscommon, another old mining area, plans are under way to protect the coal-mining heritage. The Arigna area is about 120 km (74 miles) north-west of Kilbeggan, via Mullingar, Longford and Carrick-on-Shannon.

The coal mines at Arigna closed in 1990 after 250 years of mining activity. Some of the tunnels were driven horizontally into the mountainsides for 5 km (3 miles) and there are plans to open up some of the old mine workings for visitors. Already, a series of "miners way" walks has been developed in the area and you can see for yourself where the old mines were amidst some spectacular landscapes.

Details from: **Tourist Information Office**, *Carrick-on-Shannon, Co. Leitrim; tel (078) 20170; fax (078) 20089.*

NORTH-WEST

HALF A DAY

One location, near Letterkenny in Co. Donegal, is well worth seeing as a preservation of past industry – the New Mills complex just outside the town. This consists of an old mill used for the textile trade and many other old workshops and buildings that give a very good idea of 19th-century working conditions. The whole industrial complex, beside the River Swilly, which once provided motive power to the great waterwheels, has been restored to its 19th-century condition.

New Mills, *near Letterkenny, Co. Donegal; tel (074) 25115* (open June–Sept, daily).

NORTHERN IRELAND

THREE DAYS

Throughout the North, several very fine examples of industrial archaeology can be seen. Start in Belleek, where the Belleek pottery tradition began in 1857. The old ways of working the clay, firing it and decorating it are well explained in the heritage centre and you can also see many examples of the different styles of Belleek ware from its different periods. The tour includes a fine audio-visual presentation along with a shop and restaurant.

Belleek Pottery, *Belleek, Co. Fermanagh; tel (02868) 658501* (open all year, daily).

From Belleek, travel via Derry for a total of 170 km (105 miles) to Bushmills near the north coast. Here at Bushmills, you can see the whole heritage of Bushmills whiskey, which claims to have the world's oldest distilling licence. It was established in 1608. You can enjoy an hour-long guided tour, whiskey tastings, shop and cafe.

Bushmills Distillery, *Bushmills, Co. Antrim; tel (02820) 731521; fax (02820) 73133*9 (open April–Oct, daily; Nov–March, Mon–Fri).

The other main attractions are nearer to Belfast. Pattersons Spade 5 km (3 miles) east of Templepatrick, itself 10 km (6 miles) north-west of Belfast, is the last water-powered spade mill left in Ireland. You can see the spades being made.

Pattersons, *near Templepatrick, Co. Antrim; tel (02894) 433619* (open April–Sept daily, with some exceptions).

In Belfast itself, engineering traditions manifested themselves in the construction of the Titanic at Harland & Wolff's shipyard. The ship, the leviathan of its time, sank in 1912, and its story is well known through the recent film and TV documentaries on the subject. You can follow a detailed Titanic trail through Belfast and surrounding districts. The Ulster Folk & Transport Museum at Cultra has a substantial collection of Titanic material, including photographs.

Details from: **Guidelines Tourism**, *120 Seacliff Road, Bangor, Co. Down; tel (02891) 465697; fax (02891) 454761; email shonakend@aol.com.*

From Belfast, travel 10 km (6 miles) south-west to Lisburn. In the centre of Lisburn, the Irish Linen Museum, housed in an architecturally striking new building, tells the whole story of linen making in Ireland in gripping detail with audio-visual material, photographs and artefacts. All the equipment once used, such as an 18th-century wooden beetling engine, can be seen. You can sense what the old linen mills were like and see an old spinner's cottage. It's very thorough and very rewarding. You can also get details here of the linen tours organised in the heartland of this once great industry, especially in north Co. Down.

Details from: **Tourism Information Centre**, *200 Newry Road, Banbridge, Co. Down; tel (02840) 623322; fax (02840) 623114; email banbridge@nitic.net; website www.banbridge.com.*

Irish Linen Centre, *Lisburn, Co. Antrim; tel (02892) 660038; fax (02892) 607889* (open all year, Mon–Sat).

Finally, if you travel for 10 km (6 miles) north-east of Belfast, on the main A2 road to Bangor, you will come to the real treasure of industrial heritage in the North, the Ulster Folk & Transport Museum at Cultra. It preserves everything imaginable, including old-style cottages and other buildings. Railway history is presented in great detail, with many examples of old locomotives and carriages, while the Road Transport Galleries has a great cornucopia of four-wheeled vehicles. These include bicycles, motor cycles, trams, buses, fire engines and cars. There's an interactive exhibition with Bombardier Aerospace, which tells the story of aviation, centred on Belfast, and a Titanic exhibition.

You can also see many old craft-making skills revived, such as forge work, weaving and wood turning. Among the newest attractions are the reconstruction of Carrigans Sawmill from Co. Fermanagh and the Straid corn mill, as well as a workshop from Dungannon. Altogether, it's a very full day and there are a shop and tea rooms.

New Mills complex, Letterkenny, Co. Donegal

Ulster Folk & Transport Museum, *Cultra, Co. Antrim; tel (02890) 428428; fax (02890) 428728* (open all year, daily).

TRAIL 20

Food

Ireland is renowned as a food-producing country. The more basic types of food, including pork, beef, lamb, potatoes, vegetables and dairy products, have been greatly complemented in recent years by many specialist and organic food producers. Sometimes visitors can go to the premises of a particular food producer and if you can't actually see production taking place, you can visit the shop and get details and samples of the product. While food production is scattered all over the country, certain parts are particularly prominent, including Cork, Dublin, the Mid-West and Northern Ireland.

CO. CORK

TWO DAYS

Begin your journey at the Ballymaloe Cookery School at Shanagarry, east Cork, founded in 1983 by Darina and Tim Allen – Darina is one of the country's best-known chefs and cookery writers. The Cookery School does a wide variety of courses at all levels varying in length from one day to a weekend, and up to three months in duration. You can stay here in great comfort and also explore the wonderful gardens, which include the largest herb garden in Ireland. It's worth getting their very stylishly produced programme on all their courses.
Ballymaloe Cookery School, *Kinoith, Shanagarry, Co. Cork; tel (021) 646785/646727; fax (021) 646909.*

From Ballymaloe, drive 30 km (20 miles) into Cork city. The English Market, just off Grand Parade in Cork, is an absolute mecca for food lovers. The Victorian-style market has lots of stalls run by local food producers – the display is dazzling and includes the two Cork specialities that are an acquired taste for anyone not born and bred in the county: drisheen, which is a form of tripe made from cows' intestines, and pigs' trotters.
English Market, *Cork;* (open all year, Mon–Sat 9am–5.30pm).

From Cork city, travel 25 km (15 miles) to Bandon, in West Cork. A whole range of small producers are located in West Cork, making all kinds of foods – cheeses are a speciality, but many other kinds of foods are being produced. EU regulations mean that visitors cannot go into food production areas, but in the following examples the people running the companies will discuss production, time permitting, and sell samples of their wares.

Bandon Vale Farmhouse Cheese is one of the renowned cheese makers in the district. Also in Bandon, you can visit the premises of Molaga Honey and talk about Irish honey production with Jerry and Eithne Collins, who will sell samples of their products.

From Bandon, drive the 20 km (12 miles) south-west to Clonakilty, a town renowned for its black and white puddings. While you won't be allowed to visit the production factories, you will be able to see, and perhaps purchase, the finished products in the local butchers' shops, including Twomey's.

Details from: **Fuchsia Brands Ltd**, *Shinagh House, Bandon, Co. Cork; tel (023) 41271; fax (023) 43640; email wclc@wclc.iol.ie; website www.westcorkleader.ie.*

Bandon Vale Farmhouse Cheese, *Bandon, Co. Cork; tel (023) 43334.*

Molaga Honey, *Bandon, Co. Cork; tel (023) 46208.*

Edward Twomey Victuallers, 16 Pearse Street, Clonakilty, Co. Cork; tel (023) 33365.

Over in the far west of the region, two more distinguished cheese-making concerns can be found – Durrus and Milleens. You can buy samples of the former at Durrus Cheese; while at Milleens, Veronica and Norman Steele will be happy to talk cheese with visitors, briefly, depending on their work schedule and only by arranging in advance. The setting is wonderful, at Eyeries on the far end of the Beara peninsula.

Also in this region is the West Cork Herb Farm at Skibbereen, which produces a wide variety of herbs. You can visit by arranging in advance with Rosari and Kevin O'Byrne.

Just 8 km (5 miles) east of Skibbereen is the agreeable fishing village of Union Hall. There, at the Union Hall Smoked Fish Company, John and Elmar Nolan smoke fish and if you ring in advance, it may be possible to see samples of smoked fish and to buy some delicious products. Again, everything depends on their production schedules.

Durrus Cheese, *Durrus, Co. Cork; tel (027) 61100.*
Milleens Cheese, *Eyeries, Co. Cork; tel (027) 74079.*
West Cork Herb Farm, *Skibbereen, Co. Cork; tel (028) 38428.*
Union Hall Smoked Fish Company, *Union Hall, Co. Cork; tel (028) 33125.*

MID-WEST

ONE DAY

Begin at Thurles, Co. Tipperary, at Mahers Farm at Cooleeney. Milk from the Fresian herd is used to make the most delicious Camembert-type cheese.

From Thurles, drive the 45 km (27 miles) north-west to Ballinderry, near Nenagh, to Lakeshore Foods. The factory itself is very modern, in keeping with modern food regulations, but it's fronted by an old cottage, so that it blends in environmentally. Lakeshore Foods is well known for its mustards and its other food products, such as glazes and sauces. It's a very comprehensive range, all made entirely free from artificial colourings and flavourings. You won't be able to visit the factory, but you can find out all about the company's products and buy some of their wares in the factory shop in the cottage.

From Nenagh, drive 100 km (62 miles) west, via Ennis, to Lisdoonvarna, where the Burren Smokehouse smokes all kinds of fish. It was started in 1989 by a local man, Peter Curtin and his Swedish wife, Birgitta, who "married" the fish-smoking traditions of Ireland and Sweden. Peter's family has owned the nearby Roadside Tavern for about a century and they had a long tradition of serving their own smoked salmon. Today, the main product of the Burren Smokehouse is smoked salmon, followed by smoked mackerel, trout and eel. It's one of the better organised food producers in terms of visitor facilities. People can go to their visitor centre, see how the fish is smoked, see video presentations and enjoy tastings. Staff will explain the whole process of smoking fish, because visitors cannot go into any of the production area. There's also a gourmet shop and a pub.

Mahers Farm, *Cooleeney, near Thurles, Co. Tipperary; tel (0504) 45122.*
Lakeshore Foods, *Ballinderry, near Nenagh, Co. Tipperary; tel (067) 22094/22243; fax (067) 22124* (open all year).
Burren Smokehouse, *Lisdoonvarna, Co. Clare; tel (065) 7074432; fax (065) 7074303; email burren.fish@iol.ie; website www.burrensmokehouse.ie.*

MIDLANDS AND EAST

TWO DAYS

Torc Truffles in the centre of Longford, 122 km (77 miles) north-east of Dublin, is one of several specialised chocolate producers that have been developed in Ireland. This chocolate company, which makes such delicious products as chocolate truffles and other high-quality delicacies, was started by Ruth McGarry-Quinn. It's unlikely that you will be able to see any of the production taking place, including the very skilled decorating work, but the shop has an excellent display of products and you'll be able to talk chocolate to your heart's content with the knowledgeable and enthusiastic staff.

Drive 85 km (52 miles) north-west, through Carrick-on-Shannon to Rossinver, near Manorhamilton. Here, in very wild and splendid mountain landscapes, The Organic Centre, run by Rod Alston, is Ireland's leading centre for education and information on organic farming and gardening. It's a fascinating place with a variety of gardens – you can stroll around the heritage garden and the taste garden, and see Kerry cows, ducks, geese and hens. You can also attend weekend courses, which will tell you everything you need to know about organic food growing and production. The shop has herbs and vegetables for sale, as well as organic seeds.

You can visit another very interesting organic centre at Laytown, just south of Drogheda and 40 km (25 miles) north of Dublin. It's Sonairte, the National Ecology Centre. It too does lots of courses, all designed to raise environmental awareness. On the food side, you can do a tour of the organic vegetable garden and orchard, where you can see how plants and trees are grown naturally, with pests controlled by natural means. Plants grown include beans, potatoes, pumpkins,

rhubarb and tomatoes. The centre also has an organic winery.
Torc Truffles, *Longford, Co. Longford; tel (043) 47353.*
The Organic Centre, *Rossinver, near Manorhamilton, Co. Leitrim; tel (072) 54338; fax (072) 54343; email organiccentre@eircom.net.*
Sonairte, *National Ecology Centre, The Ninch, Laytown, Co. Meath; tel (041) 9827572; fax (041) 9828130; email sonairte@drogheda.edunet.ie.*

Dublin Area

In the Dublin area, opportunities for food factory visits are limited, since the big plants, such as Cadburys, Nestlé and Tayto, do not do factory visits. Smaller food companies in Dublin generally don't have the facilities for people to come and buy their wares. However, there's one food-related place that you can visit without restriction and enjoy some priceless Dublin banter into the process. It's Moore Street, just off Henry Street, where fresh fruit and vegetables are sold off barrows. It's been a traditional shopping spot for many years and has managed to survive the depredations of development. Just the far side of Capel Street, the wholesale fruit and vegetable markets are also worth a visit, especially early in the morning. Trading normally starts around 6am, but in case you feel in need of a pick-me-up, some of the pubs have early licences, so you can have a pre-breakfast pint.
Moore Street, *Dublin; (trading all year, Mon–Sat 9am–5.30pm).*

For more information on food production in the Republic, contact the Irish Food Board: **Bord Bia,** *Clanwilliam Court, Lower Mount Street, Dublin 2; tel (01) 668 5155; fax (01) 668 7521; website www.bordbia.ie.*

Northern Ireland

One Day

The North of Ireland too has a sound reputation as a good-quality food production region, but the EU regulations are the same. Most food-making companies don't allow visitors. Until

Tandragee – 'Tayto' – Castle, Tandragee, Co. Armagh

recently, companies like Maud's Ice Cream, Larne, Co. Antrim and Cuan Sea Fisheries, Killinchy, Co. Down, had allowed visitors, but have discontinued the practice. So the number of plants that actually welcome visitors is limited.

In Portadown, 43 km (27 miles) south-west of Belfast, Irwin's Bakery was established in 1912 as a family bakery making high-quality bread and other products. It now bakes a wide range of speciality lines. The bakery is in a greenfield site, where traditional baking methods are still used. You can see many of the North's traditional breads, such as plain bread, farls and soda bread being made.

In Tandragee Castle in Co. Armagh, 10 km (6 miles) south of Portadown, the Tayto Crisps factory is on a site that includes a 17th-century castle. Tayto began production here in 1956 and the plant has steadily expanded ever since. The company makes a tasty range of crisps and other snack products and on normal working days visitor tours are arranged. The tour lasts one and a half hours and visitors must take certain precautions over footwear, and jewellery should not be worn.

Irwin's Bakery, *Diviny Drive, Carn Industrial Estate, Portadown, Co. Armagh; tel (02838) 332421; fax (02838) 333918* (tours by arrangement).

Tayto Crisps, *Tandragee Castle, Co. Armagh; tel (02838) 840249* (open Mon–Thurs, tours at l0.30am and 1.30pm; Fri, tour at 10.30am).

For further information on food production in Northern Ireland, contact: **A Taste of Ulster**, *59 North Street, Belfast; tel (02890) 231221.*

TRAIL 21

Viking Ireland

The Vikings made an enormous impact on Ireland. The three best places to explore the Viking legacy are Waterford, Limerick and Dublin. A good place to start your explorations on this three-day trail is on the website of Viking Network Ireland which has lots of detail about Viking sites in Ireland and current Viking-related activities, such as exhibitions.
Viking Network Ireland,
http//kola.dcu.ie/viking/welcome.html.

WATERFORD

ONE DAY

The earliest evidence of a permanent Viking settlement in Waterford is about AD 914, although there are various references made to Viking fleets being based in this area in the 9th century. By the 11th century, Viking Waterford had grown so much that the earthen defences were replaced by a stone wall. Reginald's Tower, on the quays, is a substantial tower built in the 13th and 14th centuries and now housing much heritage material about Waterford, but it may have been built on the site of an earlier Viking tower.

The area of Viking Waterford was actually quite small and didn't extend much beyond the area from the quays, by Reginald's Tower up to the Church of Ireland cathedral, but the legacy that the Vikings left was priceless. When excavations began in 1986 (part of the preparations for building what is now the City Square shopping centre) a huge amount of artefacts were found. The results of those excavations were certainly voluminous and the local authority has gone to great lengths to preserve and display all the material. The Viking legacy is the city's foundation.

Many of these artefacts are on show in the new Granary Exhibition Centre on the Quays. The building was converted from an old warehouse and it has several floors of exhibitions and displays that utilise the most modern electronic systems to show off the history and heritage of Waterford.

Items on display include domestic utensils, weapons and jewellery, many of which are in remarkably good condition. Much of the material, such as pottery, is impervious to the elements, but the conditions in which all this Viking material was found were so good that even wooden items have been well preserved. Prime pieces of Viking jewellery include a kite brooch, complete with fastener. The range of items is enormous, everything from spoons to candlesticks, revealing just how a Viking home would have been furnished. There's even a Viking gaming board, indication of how the Vikings entertained themselves in the long dark winter evenings. Certainly, a tour round the Waterford Treasures will give an excellent indication of what everyday life was like in Viking Waterford. **Granary Exhibition Centre**, *Waterford; tel (051) 304500; fax (051) 304501; email mail@waterfordtreasures.com; website www.waterfordtreasures.com* (open daily, all year).

If you travel 50 km (31 miles) east of Waterford (via the Passage East–Ballyhack car ferry) to Wexford, the Irish National Heritage Park has good re-creations of life in Viking times. The site depicts the various stages of settlement in Ireland from 7,000 BC up to the arrival of the Normans in the 12th century. There are plenty of authentic Viking reconstructions, with replica furniture and audio effects in each house. The park even has a replica of a Viking shipyard.

Wexford town itself was originally a Viking settlement. In fact, the name comes from Waesfjord (the harbour of the mudflats) which was the name given to the place when the Vikings arrived in AD 950. However, unlike Waterford, there's little to see today that indicates the town's Viking legacy. **Irish National Heritage Park**, *near Wexford; tel (053) 20733; fax (053) 20911; email inhp@iol.ie* (open daily, March–Oct).

LIMERICK

ONE DAY

Limerick is the other regional city in Ireland that has a strong Viking heritage. The Vikings settled on an island in the River Shannon about AD 922, but by the end of that century they had come under Irish control. Excavations on the site of King

John's Castle revealed parts of a pre-Norman wall, and in the visitor centre today you can see the preserved remains of part of the stone wall once used to fortify Viking Limerick, as well as the remains of three Viking Age houses.

King John's Castle, *Nicholas Street, Limerick; tel (061) 360788* (open daily, all year).

Dublin

One Day

Dublin was founded twice by the Vikings. The first time was in AD 841, when it was established as a centre for the lucrative slave trade. The first settlers were expelled in 902.

However, their descendants weren't slow in returning and came back to set up Dublin for the second time, in about 917. This settlement, around Wood Quay and the Christchurch Cathedral area, later developed into the modern city of Dublin. By the end of the 10th century, Dublin had become the economic focal point of the western part of the Scandinavian empire. Dublin was at the centre of the trade routes across the Atlantic and there was even trade with the eastern Mediterranean.

Extensive excavations began in 1961 and confirmed that the Vikings did in fact lay the foundations of Dublin, choosing a slope on the southside of the River Liffey, where a tributary, the Poddle, flows into the main river. In the mid 1970s, extensive excavations at Wood Quay turned up huge quantities of Viking artefacts, as well as generating considerable controversy, because Dublin Corporation planned to build new civic offices on the site.

The preservation conditions of the Viking area were remarkably good, so the artefacts that survived did so in excellent condition. Some of the Viking exhibits can be seen in the National Museum of Ireland, in Kildare Street. The Treasury display in the National Museum includes a large selection of silver and gold ornaments from the Viking Age in Ireland and are indicative of the wealth and extent of Viking settlements then.

Displayed alongside these artefacts are many examples of Irish ornaments made between the 10th and 12th centuries and heavily influenced by Viking styles. Many thousands of artefacts were excavated from the Viking town of Dublin and these are on display, including ornaments, games, domestic utensils, decorated wood, iron tools, leather and textiles, amongst many others.

House reconstructions and a model of part of the Viking town complete the display. The museum also has many artefacts found in the cemetery at Kilmainham/Islandbridge, part of the first Viking settlement in Dublin. The cemetery itself was the largest of its kind outside Scandinavia, but the only remnant still visible of the cemetery and the monastery that preceded it is a stone cross in the grounds of the Irish Museum of Modern Art at Kilmainham.

Also well worth seeing in Dublin is the Viking Adventure, at Essex Street West, off Fishamble Street. The street is situated at the far western end of Temple Bar, close to the new Dublin Corporation offices at Wood Quay. The centre has all kinds of Viking artefacts, on loan from the National Museum, and including such items as combs, knives and pins. It also has an excellent map showing what Viking Dublin would have been like in 1100. The centre has a small conservation laboratory.

Part of the centre is in an old church, which has been converted into a display and banqueting area. This used to be Adam and Eve's Church, founded in 1834. In the present banqueting area, where Viking feasts and entertainment are staged nightly, there's a modern reconstruction of a wooden Viking longship, with the side cut away. The regular tours through the centre show exactly what life was like in the Viking town of "Dyfflin". You can chat to the "locals" (present-day actors dressed as Vikings), see what daily life and work was like in Viking times and experience the sounds and smells of Viking Dublin. The latter were as strong as the Vikings' belligerent reputation.

You could also try one of the daily Viking Splash tours, which use converted amphibious vehicles to take visitors on a tour of Viking Dublin, concluding in the water at Grand Canal Basin in Ringsend. Starting point for the tours is beside the gardens at St Patrick's Cathedral.

National Museum, *Kildare Street, Dublin 2; tel (01) 661 8811; fax (01) 676 6116* (open all year, Tues–Sun).

Viking Adventure, *Essex Street West, Dublin; tel (01) 679 6040; fax (01) 679 6033* (open all year, Tues–Sat).

Viking Splash tours; *tel (01) 855 3000; website www.vikingsplashtours.com* (tours run 10 times daily from Tues–Sun; the tour time is 75 minutes).

TRAIL 22

Wildlife

This trail could take you up to two weeks.

DUBLIN

TWO DAYS

A day can be spent touring Dublin Zoo in the Phoenix Park, which has an astonishing array of animals. The zoo has been around a long time, having opened its doors in 1830; since then, many extensions have been made. It's set in some 25 hectares (63 acres) of landscaped grounds in the park, close to Áras an Uachtaráin, the official residence of the President of Ireland and the American Ambassador's residence. The park and the zoo are just 3 km (1.5 miles) from the city centre, easily reached by car or bus.

The zoo has ornamental lakes and over 700 animals and tropical birds from all over the world. The species are very wide ranging, from jaguars and snow leopards to gorillas and polar bears. Some of the more traditional zoo species are represented, including elephants and giraffes. A great variety of birds species can be found here, everything from the toucan, made famous in the old Guinness advertisements, to the Chilean flamingo and the Rodrigues fruit bat, the only mammals that can fly. Most of the animals and birds here were born and bred in zoos. Some of the species are still fairly common, but others are rare. The zoo helps to protect endangered species; the dodo, a flightless bird from Mauritius, was the most famous species to be wiped out and countless others have suffered the same fate, such as the dusky seaside sparrow, which was declared extinct as recently as 1987.

The zoo is grouped into a number of different areas, which makes it easy for visitors to find their way around. The new World of Primates has several monkey islands, while the Fringes of the Arctic section has such animals as polar bears, snowy owls and Arctic foxes. The World of Cats features jaguars, lions and snow leopards and you can also see the chimpanzees on Chimp Island. The latest addition to the zoo's facil-

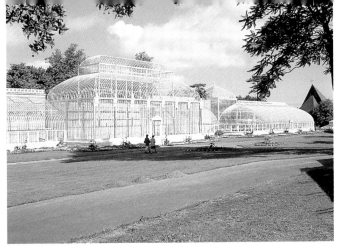

National Botanic Gardens, Glasnevin, Dublin

ities is the brand new and very large African Plains section, which houses the larger African animals, such as antelopes, bongos, giraffes, hippos and rhinos – some of the African species here have been long-time residents of the zoo.

With all the various areas, lots of information is provided about the species on display, while there's also much more material in the Discovery Centre. You can also take a train round the zoo, meet the keepers and enjoy the restaurants and the shops.

Not far from the zoo, in the Phoenix Park, the visitor centre in Ashtown Castle has lots of displays and information on the flora and fauna of the park, which was created in 1662 as a deer park. Walking around the park, the largest in Europe, you will see lots of deer.

Dublin Zoo, *Phoenix Park, Dublin; tel (01) 677 1425; fax (01) 677 1660; email info@dublinzoo.ie; website www.dublinzoo.ie* (open all year, daily).

Ashtown Castle, *Phoenix Park, Dublin; tel (01) 677 0095* (open all year, daily).

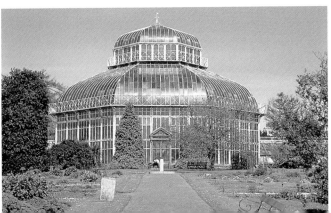

Glasshouse at the National Botanic Gardens

135

On the northside of Dublin, the National Botanic Gardens at Glasnevin, 3 km (2 miles) north of the city centre, cover a vast area beside the River Tolka. The gardens date back to 1795 and have more than 20,000 different varieties of plants, as well as a rose garden and a vegetable garden. The main man-made feature of the gardens are the wonderful curvilinear range of greenhouses. These were built by a Dublin ironmaster, Richard Turner, between 1843 and 1869 and in an arduous and most impressive restoration programme, these have now been restored to their original pristine condition.

National Botanic Gardens, *Glasnevin, Dublin; tel (01) 837 4388* (open all year, daily).

The Dublin area has a number of other important wildlife locations. Right in the city centre, St Stephen's Green is a pastoral oasis, with many ducks on the ponds. On the northside of the city, 5 km (3 miles) from the city centre, North Bull Island is an outstanding nature centre, with a great array of bird life, including mallards, moorhens and sandpipers. The island itself stretches for 5 km (3 miles) and was created by the action of the tides. It has a great expanse of sandy beach and dunes. Close by, St Anne's Park has many prize species of rose. At Rogerstown estuary, near Swords, 16 km (10 miles) north of Dublin, there's a great variety of seabirds. Also worth seeing is the Irish Seal Sanctuary at Garristown, 5 km (3 miles) west of Swords, which does sterling work in preserving the seal population around the coast.

Irish Seal Sanctuary, *Garristown, Co. Dublin; tel (01) 835 4370* (visits by arrangement).

Finally, north of Dublin, three gardens are well worth visiting. At Malahide Castle Demesne, 10 km (6 miles) north of the capital, the Talbot Botanic Gardens cover 9 hectares (23 acres). The gardens include a walled garden and many plants from the southern hemisphere.

From Malahide, drive 10 km (6 miles) east to the N1 road, then north to Newbridge Demesne. In the grounds of this Georgian manor house, there's a fine orchard garden to be explored.

From here, travel a further 8 km (5 miles) in the direction of Skerries. Just before the seaside town, follow the signs to Ardgillan Demesne. This includes a fragrant rose garden and a restored walled garden with herbs and vegetables.

On the southside of Dublin, two locations are worth visiting. The Booterstown Bird Sanctuary is alongside the main coast road to Dun Laoghaire, 6 km (4 miles) south of the city centre. It has a great array of seabirds. At Dalkey, 16 km (10 miles) south of Dublin, Dalkey Island has wildlife, including many seabirds. You can reach the island, in summer, by boat from the tiny harbour on the coast road in Dalkey.

Talbot Botanic Gardens, *Malahide, Co. Dublin; tel (01) 872 7777* (open daily, May–Sept).

Newbridge Demesne, *near Swords, Co. Dublin; tel (01) 843 6064* (open all year, daily).

Ardgillan Demesne, *near Skerries, Co. Dublin; tel (01) 849 2324* (open all year, daily).

Wexford

One Day

Wexford is 145 km (90 miles) south-east of Dublin, within two hours' driving time. It's the location of one of the most important wildlife locations in Ireland, the Wexford Slobs. These are areas of alluvial mud, north and south of the estuary, which were reclaimed in the mid l9th century and are now under crops or pasture. Both the slobs are criss-crossed by drainage ditches.

It's the most important wildfowl haunt in the Republic, supporting around 15,000 birds in winter. Nearly half the world's population of Greenland white-fronted geese winter here, when up to 10,000 can be seen. Other species to be seen here include Bewick's swans, grey plovers and mallards. There's an observation tower for viewing the reserve, while other facilities include hides and a visitor centre with an audio-visual display. The centre also has a wildfowl collection. For further information on the Wexford Slobs and other major bird sanctuaries contact BirdWatch Ireland.

Also near Wexford town, you can take a boat at the harbour in Kilmore Quay, 20 km (12 miles) south-west. The two uninhabited Saltee Islands are about 5 km (3 miles) off-shore. The habitat is totally undisturbed, making the islands a perfect "home" for about 2,000 seabirds. The trip is best done in calm summer weather.

Greenland Goose Visitor Centre, *near Wexford; tel (053) 23129; fax (053) 24785* (open all year, daily).

BirdWatch Ireland, *Ruttledge House, 8 Longford Place, Monkstown, Co. Dublin; tel (01) 280 4322; fax (01) 284 4407; email bird@indigo.ie; website www.birdwatchireland.ie.*

CORK

TWO DAYS

From Wexford, drive 193 km (120 miles) west to Cork. En route, stop off in the seaside town of Dungarvan, "capital" of west Waterford. The bay is a broad sweep of shallow water, with the inner part of the bay divided by the Cunnigar sand spit. This is the best place in the estuary for lots of seabird species, including terns.

Just east of Cork, turn off the main N25 at Carrigtwohill for Fota Wildlife Park. The park has over 90 exotic species, many of them endangered, such as cheetahs, lion-tailed macaques and oryx. The primary aim of Fota Park is the conservation and breeding of endangered species. There is a gift shop and cafe.

Fota Arboretum, Carrigtwo-hill, Co. Cork

On the same estate, you can also visit the Fota Arboretum and Gardens, which have an extensive collection of trees and shrubs on over 11 hectares (27 acres). These gardens were laid out in the early 19th century by James Hugh Smith Barry and contain many plant examples from the southern hemisphere. It will take between one and two hours to explore the gardens.

On the southside of Cork city, it's worth going to a place called The Lough. From the city centre head southwards for 3 km (2 miles) in the direction of Togher. The Lough is a large man-made lake and it's home to an amazing variety of ducks and other species.

Fota Wildlife Park, *Carrigtwohill, Co. Cork; tel (021) 4812678; fax (021) 4812744* (open daily, March–Sept; Oct–Dec, Sat–Sun).

Fota Arboretum and Gardens, *Carrigtwohill, Co. Cork; tel (021) 4812728; fax (021) 481278* (open daily, April–Oct).

Travelling westwards from Cork, several other locations have important bird reserves. Kinsale Marsh, 32 km (20 miles) south-west of Cork city, is on the Bandon River estuary and it has large numbers of wintering wildfowl. It also has lots of other species, such as cormorants, curlews and herons, all of which can be seen from the causeway. Twenty-five km (15 miles) south-west of Kinsale, on the eastern side of Clonakilty Bay, Flaxford Pond is a small freshwater lake and reedbed separated from the sea by the coast road. Many waders and wildfowl come here and there's a heronry nearby. You can see the birds from the public road.

Finally, in West Cork, it's worth taking the ferry from Baltimore out to Cape Clear Island. The island has an abundance of natural attractions, it's an Irish-speaking stronghold, and is also famed for its seabird life.

Co. Kerry

Two Days

Kerry is one of the best wildlife habitats in Ireland and two centres in particular are worth exploring. Off Waterville, the

Skelligs (Great and Small) are wonderfully bleak. The larger island has the remains of a 7th-century monastery close to its summit; the ruins are approached by climbing hundreds of steps. The island towers 218 metres (714 ft) above sea level, so it's a truly daunting climb. The Skelligs also have a wonderful assortment of seabirds and you can see them for yourself if you visit the island. You can find out much about their habitats in the Skellig Experience Heritage Centre on nearby Valentia Island, including a 16-minute audio-visual show. As part of the visit to the centre you can take an organised boat trip, seeing the Skelligs from the relative comfort of the cruising boat.

You can also take a boat trip out to Puffin Island, 7 kms (4 miles) due south of Bray Head on Valentia Island. Colonies of puffins number between 5,000 and 10,000, while there are also large colonies of Manx shearwaters, besides guillemots, kittiwakes, razorbills and storm petrels.

Puffin Island boat trip, *contact Des Lavelle, (066) 9476306.*
Skellig Experience Heritage Centre, *Valentia Island, Co. Kerry; tel (066) 9476306* (open daily, all year).

The other great natural attraction in Co. Kerry is of course Fungi the dolphin in Dingle Harbour. The playful dolphin has been resident here for many years and you can take a boat trip out from the harbour to see Fungi in action. For a more detailed tour, you can do a Dingle Marine Eco-Tour from Dingle Pier. The boat will cruise around Dingle Bay and then around the coastline of the Dingle peninsula. The sights are incredible, including cliffs full of nesting seabirds, such as cormorants, guillemots, razorbills, shags and terns. You are likely to see many seals around the coastline – the warm waters of the Gulf Stream encourage them – and sometimes schools of dolphins, not to mention pods of orca whales.

The Dingle area is a veritable treasure trove of rare fish species and 90 per cent of all the rare fish recorded in the National Museum of Ireland have been landed at Dingle. The Dingle Oceanworld, which was opened in 1998, is a very modern aquarium that reflects this rich heritage. It has a specially designed shark tank full of natural seawater and a bevy of these most feared creatures of the sea. Other features include an estuary section, a harbour section and a touch pool, where visitors can interact with such species as brill, plaice, rays and turbot. You can, for instance, stroke the large rays along the sides of their wings, an experience they seem to enjoy. You can also see the box crab, the largest crab to live off the Irish coast. The Wave Tank simulates natural offshore conditions, while you can walk through the Ocean Tunnel to see the latest arrivals. It's a very comprehensive and well-presented display.

Dingle Marine Eco-Tours, *Dingle Pier, Co. Kerry; tel (086) 2858802.*

The Dingle Oceanworld (Mara Beo), *Dingle, Co. Kerry; tel (066) 9152111; fax (066) 9152155; email marabeo@iol.ie; website www.dingle-oceanworld.ie* (open all year, daily).

SHANNON ESTUARY

ONE DAY

From the delights of Dingle, drive northwards to the Shannon estuary, taking the car ferry from Tarbert to Killimer. From Kilrush, drive 25 km (15 miles) over narrow roads to Carrigaholt. This is close to Loop Head, at the far end of the northern side of the estuary.

Dolphinwatch Carrigaholt uses a new, custom-built boat to take visitors out to see the dolphins. A large group of bottlenose dolphins, over 100 in all, live in the Shannon estuary and their playful and inquisitive instincts can be observed from the boat. You can also see the seabird life of the Loop Head peninsula, which is one of the main sites in Europe for common and migratory seabirds.

Dolphinwatch, *Carrigaholt, Co. Clare; tel (065) 9058156; email dwatch@iol.ie; website www.dolphinwatch.ie* (trips operated April–Oct).

GALWAY

ONE DAY

Galway Bay and Lough Corrib are rich in birdlife. Galway Bay is a very wide bay, about 10 km (6 miles) wide, and at several points around its shores you will see many examples of birdlife.

The Galway city rubbish dump, just north of the city, is a rich breeding ground for several species of gulls. Tawin Island, on the eastern shores of the bay, close to Clarinbridge, is excellent for seeing geese. On the northern shores of the bay, starting in Galway docks and moving on through Salthill with its beach, you will see many examples of gulls. During the winter, typical wintering waders, such as oystercatchers, can be easily seen.

Inland from Galway and starting just north of the city, the great expanse of Lough Corrib is home to countless bird species, including winter wildfowl from August to February. The islands on the lake have big colonies of breeding gulls. You really need a boat to explore this vast expanse of water; it's often difficult to find vantage points along the shoreline.

Co. Mayo

Two Days

Three locations provide lots of wildlife excitement. The easiest to reach is Achill Island, where the great cliffs are home to countless seabirds. Clare Island requires a rather arduous boat journey from Roonagh Quay, near Louisburgh, but once you are there it's a good place to stay for the bird-watching. The spectacular cliffs on the north side of the island have such birds as kittiwakes, while other birds, including puffins, are there in smaller numbers. Finally, the two low, windswept, uninhabited Inishkea Islands, off the southern part of the Mullet peninsula, are exceptionally difficult to reach, only done by concluding a deal with a local boatman. The islands are home to many geese, while grey seals are abundant.

Co. Donegal

Two Days

This county has some of the richest birdlife in the country. Its coastline and inland lakes are perfect breeding grounds. In the east of the county, Lough Swilly has a dense population of wintering wildfowl and waders; one of the best vantage points is Inch Island, opposite Fahan, which is renowned for its geese species. Inch is worth seeing for its birdlife at any time of the year; you may even hear that rare and endangered species, the corncrake.

In the far west of the county, it's worth exploring Sheskinmore Lough, which is approached by turning off the main road north from Ardara to Rosbeg. It's a shallow lake that has breeding waders in summer and big flocks of geese in winter. It's an internationally important wetland, also noted for wild flowers.

In the far north of the county, Horn Head has some of the most spectacular cliffs in Ireland – a good match for Slieve League in south-west Donegal. The cliffs at Horn Head are a major breeding ground for seabirds, while they are also the principal breeding site in Ireland for razorbills. Finally, if you want a really isolated, often storm-tossed trip, go to Malin Head at the far north of the Inishowen peninsula. At the tiny harbour near Malin Head, you may be able to arrange with a local fisherman to take you the 10 km (6 miles) across to the deserted island of Inishtrahull, entirely peaceful and utterly relaxing, besides being a good vantage point for seabirds.

Northern Ireland

Two Days

The North of Ireland has some very interesting wildlife locations and it's best to start in Belfast with the zoo. Its origins date back to early in the 20th century, when the horse-drawn trains extended out to Whitewell and Glengormley. In 1911, the line was taken over by Belfast Corporation, which then decided to develop the Bellevue Gardens as a playground and pleasure gardens. In 1934, 4.85 hectares (12 acres) was laid out as a zoo. In the 1950s and 1960s, the zoo went into decline and in 1974, the new development of Belfast Zoo was started. So in recent years a completely new zoo has been built, replicating as far as possible the conditions of the wild.

The zoo has many interesting collections, including African birds and animals such as cheetahs, meerkats, African wild dogs and black-footed cats from the Kalahari desert. Gazelles, giraffes and zebras as well as monkeys also feature from Africa, which provides one of the strong points of the collection. From Asia come many species of birds and animals such as tigers and the Malayan sun bear, the smallest of the bear family. South America is well represented with the likes of the Columbian spider monkey, marmosets and tamarins. From North America comes the Californian sea lion, while from Antarctica come the penguins. Australia presents such delights as the kangaroo and the wallaby.

The collection, from all continents, is very impressive indeed, but there are also animals from nearer home. The zoo has a farm of rare breeds, which includes Galway sheep and Irish moiled (hornless) cattle. There is also a mountain tea shop, a restaurant and a souvenir shop.

Belfast Zoo, *Belfast; tel (02890) 776277; fax (02890) 370578* (open all year, daily).

Close to the zoo is the Cave Hill Country Park, with plenty of natural attractions. You can climb up Cave Hill to MacArt's Fort on the top, where United Irishmen helped plan the 1798 rebellion.

Other parks in the Belfast area with plenty of flora and fauna include the Sir Thomas and Lady Dixon Park on the Upper Malone Road in south Belfast, which is one of the world's best rose gardens, the woodlands and walks of Minnowburn Beeches, again in south Belfast, and the Colin Glen Forest Park in west Belfast. The Colin Glen Park covers 89 hectares (200 acres) and has nature trails and wildlife ponds. The visitor centre has audio-visual presentations.

Colin Glen Park, *Belfast; tel (02890) 614115* (open all year, daily).

From Belfast, travel 45 km (27 miles) south-east to Portaferry, on the eastern shores of Strangford Lough. The Exploris Aquarium is an excellent presentation of the marine life of the lough and the Irish Sea. It also has a new seal sanctuary.

At Seaforde, 25 km (15 miles) west of Portaferry (take the Strangford ferry and go through Downpatrick), the Seaforde Gardens have hundreds of free-flying exotic butter-flies, as well as reptiles and insects, rare plants and parrots.

Exploris Aquarium, *Portaferry, Co. Down; tel (02842) 728062* (open all year, daily).

Seaforde Gardens, *Seaforde, Co. Down; tel (02844) 811225* (open daily, Easter–Sept).

Lough Neagh

One Day

Lough Neagh, the great inland lake in the centre of the North, has many wildlife attractions around its shores. These include the eel fishery at Toome on the north-east corner and, at the opposite end of the lake, Oxford Island and the Lough Neagh Discovery Centre. This centre details, in a visitor-friendly way, the wildlife, history and management of both the immediate Oxford Island area and the broader perspective of Lough Neagh. The centre has interactive exhibitions, a shop and cafe, while outside, 8 km (5 miles) of walks have been laid out.

Peatlands Park, at Dungannon, is 20 km (12 miles) west of the Lough Neagh Discovery Centre. The park was the first of its kind in these islands to highlight issues relating to peatland; it is crossed by paths and boardwalks and has a narrow gauge railway.

Go 20 km (12 miles) north to Kinturk Cultural Centre, which is on the western shores of Lough Neagh, close to Ardboe. The whole history of the Lough Neagh fishing industry, including those all important eels, is explained and documented, complete with displays of old traditional boats and fishing gear. You can also take a boat trip and guided tour, and there is a restaurant.

Lough Neagh Discovery Centre, *near Lurgan, Co. Armagh; tel (02838) 322205* (open April–Sept, daily; Oct–March, Wed–Sun).

Peatlands Park, *Dungannon, Co. Tyrone; tel (02838) 851102* (open all year, daily).

Kinturk Cultural Centre, *Ardboe, Co. Tyrone; tel (02886) 736512* (open all year, daily).

TRAIL 23

Potteries

Potteries are an integral part of the crafts movement in Ireland, with hundreds of them established all over the country. In order to be selective, a limited number have been chosen for this six-day tour, including the top name potteries such as Belleek, Louis Mulcahy and Stephen Pearce.

ENNISCORTHY

ONE DAY

The best place to begin any tour of potteries in Ireland is in Enniscorthy, Co. Wexford, where the craft began in Ireland. Carley's Bridge Potteries, 2 km (1 mile) west of the town, is the oldest pottery in Ireland. It was founded in 1654 by two brothers from Cornwall in south-west England, where there's a long history of china clay mining and pottery making. The Carley brothers arrived in Enniscorthy and decided to set up the pottery close to a suitable deposit of clay. They found an excellent clay source and founded their pottery nearby; it continues to this day. However, about six generations ago, one of the women of the Carley family married a man called Owens, so the family name of the owners of the pottery has been Owens ever since.

The pottery is famous for its long tradition, stretching back over 300 years, of making earthenware products. Many of the products made originally in the pottery, such as bricks, drainage pipes, country kitchenware and tiles can still be seen in old farmhouses in Co. Wexford. Both the County Museum in Enniscorthy and the Agricultural Museum at Johnston Castle, Co. Wexford, have many examples of wares made by the Carley's Bridge Potteries. It has also made earthenware plant pots for a long time.

In more recent times, there's been a big revival of interest in hand-made clay flowerpots, so these are now an important part of the production schedule. If you visit the pottery, you can see how the clay is moulded into pots on the potter's wheel. Throwing a pot takes as little as a minute; each product made is stamped with the words "Carley's Bridge Potteries, est. 1654 Enniscorthy".

The beehive-shaped coal-fired kiln used for firing the pots is considered to be the largest used for hand-made pots in Ireland. It can hold up to 30,000 and it takes up to three months to make enough pots to fill the kiln. Actually stacking the kiln takes three days, then the kiln is ready to be fired. The temperature is raised to 1000 degrees centigrade over a period of two days, then it takes a further two days for it to be cool enough for the products to be taken out. You can follow the whole fascinating process.

Another smaller, but equally traditional pottery, the Hillview Pottery, is nearby and can be visited throughout the week. It's been run at his home here by Paddy Murphy since 1980.

A complete contrast is provided by the nearby Kiltrea Bridge Pottery, on the R702 road just west of Enniscorthy. Kiltrea Bridge produces very modern kitchen and interior items, as well as terracotta patio pots, all with very stylish designs and glazes, reflecting contemporary European tastes in pottery. Unlike the other local potteries, Kiltrea Bridge blends clays from all over Ireland, as far away as Co. Tipperary and Co. Tyrone.

These three potteries are grouped together in the same area west of the town. Bill Connor's Badger Hill Pottery is to the immediate south of the town, off the N79 to New Ross. His cookware and ornamental pots are more exotic in design, reflecting his years of travel around the world.

Carley's Bridge Potteries, *Enniscorthy, Co. Wexford; tel (054) 33512; fax (054) 34360* (open all year, Mon–Fri; also Sat–Sun in summer).

Hillview Pottery, *Enniscorthy, Co. Wexford; tel (054) 35443* (open daily).

Kiltrea Bridge Pottery, *Enniscorthy, Co. Wexford; tel (054) 35107; fax (054) 34690* (open all year, Mon–Sat and bank holiday weekends).

Badger Hill Pottery, *Enniscorthy, Co. Wexford; tel (054) 35060* (open Wed–Sun; Mon by arrangement).

KILKENNY

ONE DAY

From Enniscorthy, drive 72 km (46 miles) to Kilkenny, via New Ross, a very picturesque route. Kilkenny is at the very heart of craft making in Ireland and you can see excellent and varied examples of pottery made in and around the city in the Kilkenny Design Centre, opposite the castle.

One of the most renowned of the Kilkenny potters is Nicholas Mosse, whose pottery is in Bennettsbridge, an attractive village set beside the River Nore, 8 km (5 miles) south-east of Kilkenny. Nicholas Mosse makes brightly coloured earthenware from Irish clay and decorates them with traditional motifs inspired by old Irish spongeware. The pottery has a visitor centre in its recently renovated mill. On the bottom level, visitors can get a good look at how the pottery is hand-made, finished and decorated. There's a shop attached, for buying what has been described as the world's largest selection of traditionally based Irish spongeware. The designs produced are quirky and interesting, always capturing the interest of the end user. Nicholas Mosse pottery has often been featured internationally and it's held in high esteem.

Also in the same village of Bennettsbridge is Stoneware Jackson Pottery, which produces a wide range of ware, from large platters to table lamps. The pots are hand-made and are glazed in colours and textures that bring out the vitality and tactile qualities of the soft clay. Visitors can watch the craftspeople at work and browse in the showrooms.

Someone who trained in pottery in Co. Kilkenny, on the Crafts Council of Ireland pottery skills course in Thomastown, was Lucy Dolan. She went on to set up her own pottery at Screggan, just outside Tullamore. With her, the Celtic influence is strong, including design inspiration from Celtic architecture, artefacts and manuscripts. Each piece is hand-thrown with a rough stoneware clay and individually decorated by cutting, rouletting and press-moulding.

Kilkenny Design Centre, *Kilkenny; tel (056) 22118* (open all year, Mon–Sat 9am–6pm, Sun 10am–6pm except Jan).

Nicholas Mosse, *Bennettsbridge, Co. Kilkenny; tel (056) 27505; fax (056) 27491; email sales@nicholasmosse.ie; website*

www.NicholasMosse.com (open all year, daily).
Stoneware Jackson Pottery, *Bennettsbridge, Co. Kilkenny; tel (056) 27275; fax (056) 27493* (open all year, Mon–Sat).
Lucy Dolan, *Screggan, Tullamore, Co. Offaly; tel (0506) 21218; email lucyceramics@hotmail.com.*

CO. CORK

ONE DAY

From Bennettsbridge, drive 145 km (90 miles) south-west, through Waterford and Dungarvan, to Shanagarry in east Cork. This is the location for another of Ireland's most renowned potteries, the Stephen Pearce Pottery, on the edges of Ballycotton Bay. The pottery owes its origins to Stephen Pearce's father, Philip, who decided in the 1940s to change from being a printer to being a potter.

He and his wife Lucy came to Shanagarry from Britain and set up the pottery in 1953, producing what became the renowned Shanagarry range of earthenware pottery. Stephen, the eldest of the three Pearce children, started his apprenticeship as a potter in 1963, in both stoneware and earthenware, studying in England and France. In 1966, on scholarship, he spent a year in Japan, studying with one of that country's most famous potters, Kanhesaige Toyo. He then spent some years travelling, before he returned to Shanagarry and opened his own pottery. He started to create what many observers consider is Ireland's best-known pottery range, "The Traditional Terracotta and White". In 1987, he introduced his second range, "Celebration". It incorporates the great Chinese and Japanese tradition of blue decoration. In 1993, he revitalised the Shanagarry range and two years later, acquired Carrigaline pottery. Carrigaline in east Cork, near Shanagarry, is a town steeped in the pottery tradition which goes back 250 years in this part of the county. Other attractions attached to the pottery include Shanagarry Castle, a maze and a cafe.
Stephen Pearce Pottery, *Shanagarry, Co. Cork; tel (021) 646807; fax (021) 646706* (open all year, daily).

From Shanagarry, drive 64 km (40 miles) west, through Cork city, to Bandon. Here, Jane Forrester and her team of potters produce a range of very colourful stoneware pots, designed for kitchen and dining table use. Bandon Pottery was originally set up in 1978 as R & S Forrester, to make and sell hand-made pottery at its premises in North Main Street, Bandon. Its unique Apple design motif soon attracted widespread interest. In a reorganisation in 1996, Jane Forrester, a director of the company, moved production to two industrial units on an industrial estate in the town and a retail unit in the town, at St Finbarr's Place. With the move to further new premises in 1999, the new Lauragh range of high-fired stoneware was introduced, featuring five different colourways – it's a very dynamic pottery.

Bandon Pottery, *Bandon, Co. Cork; tel (023) 41360; fax (023) 41287; email trade@bandonpottery.ie; website: www.bandonpottery.ie* (open all year, daily).

Louis Mulcahy Pottery, Ballyferriter, Dingle, Co. Kerry

Throughout the West Cork region, you'll find many small potteries. Details from: **Tourist Information Office**, *Skibbereen; tel (028) 21766; fax (028) 23153.*

CO. KERRY

TWO DAYS

From Bandon, drive 168 km (105 miles) north-west to Killarney, through the towns of Clonakilty, Skibbereen, Bantry and Kenmare.

In the grounds of Muckross House just outside Killarney, in a walled garden crafts centre, you'll find Margaret Phelan's Mucros Pottery. She has been making pottery here for the past 16 years, having moved to Killarney from Mayo. The pottery, which employs four people, makes a wide variety of items, including plates and lamps. The design is very detailed and the tableware and gift ware is produced in a distinctive honey and blue glaze. Visitors are welcome at the studios to see the craftspeople in action.

Mucros Pottery, *Killarney, Co. Kerry; tel (064) 31440; fax (064) 33926; email mucros@iol.ie; website www.muckross-house.ie* (open Mon–Sat, all year).

From Killarney, drive 96 km (60 miles) through Tralee and Dingle, to Ballyferriter on the western edge of the Dingle peninsula. Few potteries can have such a scenic situation, right on the edge of the Atlantic and fewer can have a higher reputation for artistic standards than Louis Mulcahy. His Potadóireacht na Caolóige has a worldwide reputation. He and his wife started the pottery 30 years ago and that two-person operation has grown to one employing around 50. After he won first place in the pottery section in the National Crafts Competition in 1975, he decided to relocate his workshop from Dublin to Dingle. The aim was to produce the best possible products, aesthetically and technically.

The pottery is one of the last big potteries to work exclusively in the traditional hand-made tradition and this is what distinguishes it from mechanically made pottery. The pottery is particularly renowned for its rich, lustrous glazes, devised and developed by Louis Mulcahy. He is also responsible for designing every piece. Such is the reputation of the pottery that every November and early December, when many of the local guesthouses and rented accommodation would be closed for the winter, they are kept open to cater for the large numbers of people who come to the annual sale. The pottery produces an enormous range of functional ware, as well as decorative items on a large scale.

Potadóireacht na Caolóige, *Ballyferriter, Co. Kerry; tel (066) 9156229/9156429; fax (066) 9156366; email clothar@mulcahy-pottery.ie.* (open all year, daily). Louis Mulcahy also has a shop on Dublin's Dawson Street, *tel (01) 670 9311.*

CO. DONEGAL

ONE DAY

In the north-west of Ireland, two potteries located within 8 km (5 miles) of each other will provide a useful day's tour. In Ballyshannon, Donegal Parian China makes a wide selection of products. The company was established in 1986 to make Parian china, which derives its name from the Greek island of Paros, because of the similarity between the china and the marble that was once quarried on the island. Parian china is much lighter and much more translucent than bone china, but unlike bone china, it cannot be machine-made in any way. Each Parian china piece has to be individually made. Moulding and firing the individual pieces requires great care and skill, while the final decoration and hand painting comes before the piece is fired for the third and final time. The products cover many giftware, tableware and unique basketware items. The craftworkers continue a great tradition that began originally in the potteries in the English Midlands, which began to make Parian china in the 1840s.

At the visitor centre in Donegal Parian, people can see an audio-visual presentation on the production process, then tour the factory. The company, now owned by Belleek, employs around 80 people and attracts over 100,000 visitors a year.

Donegal Parian China, *Ballyshannon, Co. Donegal; tel (072) 51826; fax* (072) 51122; email donchina@indigo.ie (open all year, daily).

It's only a short journey from Ballyshannon across to Belleek, which is just in Co. Fermanagh. The pottery here has worldwide renown. It was set up in 1857 and like Donegal Parian, it too produces fine quality Parian china. When the founder of the firm, John Caldwell Bloomfield, started up, he pledged that any piece with even the slightest flaw would be destroyed. That golden rule has been adhered to ever since.

Belleek products continue to be entirely hand-made, finely decorated and finished. The firm itself has been through cyclical periods in its fortunes, and different ownerships, but today it is thriving as never before. The various periods of Belleek have their own admirers and many of the earlier pieces fetch enormous prices. The visitor centre offers tours, where people can get a behind-the-scenes look at the master crafts-men at work, as they have been for a century and half, making the delicate eggshell china. They use the same methods and techniques that have always been used. The secrets of making Belleek are first unveiled in the casting and fettling shops, fol-lowed by the flowering room, where the Parian ware is designed, moulded and shaped. It's quite incredible to see the craftsmen weaving the delicate and intricate strands of the bas-ketware and watching them create tiny petals, stems and twigs. The tour concludes with a visit to the furnace area, where the pieces are fired, and then the painting rooms, where the fin-ishing touches are applied to individual pieces.

As well as this factory tour, the video presentation in the theatre explains the complicated history of Belleek. Visitors can also admire some of the oldest and rarest pieces of Belleek, as well as perhaps buying their own. The centre also has an award-winning restaurant.

Belleek Pottery, *Belleek, Co. Fermanagh; tel (02868) 658501* (tours Mon–Fri, centre open daily).

The above are the main potteries in Ireland, but all over the country many smaller ones exist – Co. Wicklow, for instance, has a profusion. At Carlingford, Celtic Clays produces a range of hand-thrown domestic stoneware, decorated with Celtic designs. The reduction firing enriches the unique glazes, to give them an antiquated look. In Westport, Co. Mayo, Roger Harley has been running his very distinctive Absolutely Pottery since 1994. It's close to the Octagon in central Westport. The domestic stoneware is hand-made in all sorts of unusual

Belleek Pottery, Belleek, Co. Fermanagh

designs and colourways. Altogether, in the whole of Ireland, there are about 250 potters operating businesses, so you won't be stuck for choice wherever you are.

Another useful address is the Home Thrown group, which includes such well-known potteries as Louis Mulcahy and Stoneware Jackson. The group exists to promote the profile of Irish hand-made pottery.

Celtic Clays, *Riverlane, Carlingford, Co. Louth; tel (042) 9383996.*

Home Thrown, *4 Mincloon, Clybaun Road, Galway; tel/fax (091) 528524; email hmorley@esatclear.ie; website www.home-thrown.com.*

For more information on potteries, contact: **Crafts Council of Ireland**, *Castle Yard, Kilkenny; tel (056) 61804; fax (056) 63754; email ccoi@craftscouncil-of-ireland.ie; website wwww.craftscouncil-of-ireland.ie.*

TRAIL 24

Contemporary Musicians and Writers

DUBLIN

Dublin has a great reputation for producing singers, songwriters and plain ordinary writers of prose and poetry. During the past 20 years, the city has seen a veritable explosion of creative talent in the musical and literary spheres and a whole galaxy of names, from U2 to Roddy Doyle, have been world-renowned, giving the city a global status in these fields just as much as Joyce and Yeats did in their time. The enormous economic expansion of Dublin in the past two decades has run in parallel with this vast creative upsurge and it looks as if the two have been deeply symbiotic. A number of readily identifiable sites around the city can be visited, some with care because they are less salubrious districts, but interesting nonetheless.

To start the music playing first, the best place to begin is right in the city centre, at the Hot Press Irish Music Hall of Fame in Middle Abbey Street, just off its intersection with O'Connell Street. This is much more than a live performance venue, with daily shows by top-line Irish and international talent. Recent artists to have appeared there include Divine Comedy, David Bowie, Moloko and Sinéad O'Connor. It's an excellent performance venue, but much more than that, its an interactive museum of Irish pop music in all its facets. You may be surprised to be confronted by a very lifelike full-sized wax model of a former Taoiseach (Prime Minister), Albert Reynolds. He is not there for any political reasons, but because he began his career promoting showbands, proving himself to be a musical entrepreneur par excellence.

In the 1960s, the whole music revolution started to roll in Ireland, not just with the showband stuff but with folk singing too. In the mid 1960s, lots of showbands were touring the country, with artists like Brendan Bowyer belting out this new sound and drawing huge crowds to ballrooms all over the country. "The Huckle Buck" and numerous other dashing ditties were top of the pops; alongside this musical phenomenon, the folk stuff was beginning, in places like O'Donoghue's pub in Merrion Row and the Abbey Tavern in Howth. At the same time, a complete metamorphosis of Irish traditional music was being wrought in an incredibly unique and magical way by Seán Ó Riada. The 1960s were hip-hop times, musically and economically, that twin theme once again. You can see a very realistic Joe Dolan, in his inevitable white suit, one of the musical icons of the 1960s and still going full throttle in 2001. The museum is excellent, because it makes use of all media; you can see lots of artefacts connected with the great musicians and songwriters, you can see videos of their performances and listen to the audio cassette as you tour round.

The '60s saw the formation of the Dubliners, while in the '70s, Celtic music was dragged into the 20th century when Horslips merged Irish traditional music with hard rock. Then punk shook the city and the Boomtown Rats kicked off in 1975. All the sounds of the past four decades are encapsulated here. Visitors find the whole experience engrossing and it's a great introduction to the whole world of contemporary musicians and singers, the likes of U2, Rory Gallagher, Phil Lynott (whose death in 1986 was a watershed for music), the Boomtown Rats with the now knighted Bob Geldof, Sinéad O'Connor... the list goes on and on. All the "greats" are there and it isn't just rock and roll. The big names of folk are pasted up there in the lights, Mary Black, Dolores Keane, Eleanor McEvoy.

Every type of music has experienced the damburst effect in Ireland: classical, jazz, folk, rock and roll, garage and the entire spectrum of so-called pop music is well covered at the Music Hall of Fame. Even if you have just a passing interest in the subject, you'll come out of the place bebopping, but if you've a more specialist interest, then all the material is here.

In the heart of Temple Bar you can go to the Bad Ass Café in Crown Alley. In 1982, Sinéad O'Connor, the wild bisexual shoot-your-mouth-off singer made her musical debut at the age of 14. She co-wrote a single for a Dublin rock band, Tua Nua, and sang the piece. Then she joined an outfit called Ton Ton Macoute and it was while she was with this band that she day-jobbed as a waitress in the Bad Ass Café. Then her 1987 LP "The Lion and the Cobra" made her a star and her shaved head and waif-like appearance world famous.

From here, you could pay a reverential visit to the offices of Hot Press at Trinity Street, just off Dame Street (just 500 metres across the River Liffey from the Music Hall of Fame), and buy a shiny new copy of the now square-shaped magazine, which is anything but square, as it continues to be the Bible to the musical business. It was launched in 1977, and has charted the rise (and sometimes fall) of every big name in the business in Ireland. Many top acts have written pieces for the magazine, including Bono and Adam (U2), Elvis Costello, Enya, Bob Geldof and Noel Redding (Jimi Hendrix Experience). The magazine isn't just about music, it also covers lots of social and political issues. It's a perceptive guide through the jungle of contemporary Dublin.

Street performance, Grafton Street, Dublin

Hot Press Irish Music Hall of Fame, *57 Middle Abbey Street, Dublin 1; tel (01) 878 3345; fax (01) 878 2225; website www.imhf.com.*
Hot Press, *13 Trinity Street, Dublin 1; tel (01) 679 5077.*
From the Hot Press offices, take a casual stroll up into Suffolk Street, passing the Dublin Tourism offices en route, into Grafton Street.

Grafton Street has some great live performances and perhaps some of the stars of the future are here, strumming away. One of the groups that did begin here were the Furey Brothers and Davey Arthur. They grew up in the working-class suburb of Ballyfermot, part of the first generation of Irish travelling people to live in fixed homes. Their traveller roots have been wellsprings for the four brothers giving them bountiful songs, stories and tunes. The brothers and their friend, Davey Arthur, finally pushed their way into the commercial mainstream in the early 1980s with such hits as "The Green Fields of France". The lads still have a great reputation for carousing and revelling, creating a raucous blitz just as effectively as any rock band.

Up near the top of Grafton Street is Captain America's restaurant, going strong since the 1960s. A former Trinity College student, Chris de Burgh, began his musical career here in the early 1970s by singing for his supper and to customers enjoying theirs, going on to achieve superstar status in the late 1980s with such songs as "Lady in Red". Another cafe in Grafton Street, Bewleys, has lots of musical connotations, because it was here that Bob Geldof and his fellow Boomtown Rats met in their early days to plan gigs and songs. One of the early classics, "Rat Trap", was created right here in Bewleys. While the Boomtown Rats themselves melted down in the late 1980s, Bob Geldof ("King Rat") goes on, better known now as multimillionaire entrepreneur and sometime saint. For him, the two co-mingle.

Just off Grafton Street, in Duke Street, you can take refreshments in The Duke pub, considered by some to be the spiritual home of the Hothouse Flowers, those irrepressible prophets of Gaeldom. Their lead singer, Liam O'Maonlai has strong traditional musical roots and is a Sean-Nós (old-style) singer of great renown. Other members of the group are as familiar with the Fleadh Cheoil as The Fender Strat.

At the top of Grafton Street is South King Street and the renowned Gaiety Theatre. It's a grand old lady of Irish theatre, one of only three Victorian/Edwardian theatres left in the country, and recently much refurbished. It's also been the setting for many memorable performances by such top musicians as Christy Moore. In the 1960s, he was touring on the folk circuit in Britain, returning home to Ireland in 1970. Soon afterwards, he became a key element in Planxty, which could be considered one of the most influential traditional and folk groups of them all. In the 1980s, Moore moved on to the Moving Hearts. But it was as a solo artist that he had the greatest impact and the Gaiety Theatre was greatly associated with his stunning performances, just as the Olympia Theatre in Dame Street is indelibly linked with that tremendous folk singer, Mary Black.

From the Olympian heights of the Gaiety, it's time to move on, just 300 metres, past the august Shelbourne Hotel into Merrion Row. O'Donoghue's pub here was one of, if not the, cornerstone of the folk music business in Ireland. The Dubliners started the whole thing; they were originally called the Ronnie Drew Group and they came together around 1962 in the back bar of O'Donoghue's. They went from success to success, with much more than "Seven Drunken Nights", so much so that 25 years later they were back in the international charts alongside their direct musical descendants, The Pogues, singers of the "Irish Rover". One of the Dubliners who made a huge impact was the diminutive and sandpaper-voiced Luke Kelly, who died tragically young in 1984 after years of heavy drinking. But what a legacy from him and the rest of the Dubliners; performers as diverse as Bono, Phil Lynott and Shane McGowan were all deeply influenced by them.

Just along the street from O'Donoghue's, you are into Lower Baggot Street where there's another pub of great musical renown, the Baggot Inn. When the Moving Hearts were formed in 1981, they fused traditional music, jazz and blues to form a unique rock beat. They lasted as a group for just three years and patrons of the Baggot Inn had some fiery pounding sounds from them. Another noted musical venue in the city worth going to for live shows is Whelans in Wexford Street.

From O'Connell Bridge, go down the Liffeyside quays, opposite the Custom House, for 1 km (0.6 mile) as far

Bewley's Café, Grafton Street, Dublin

as Windmill Lane. These are the famous recording studios and outside them you can see the famous wall covered with fans' graffiti, inspired by U2, who have often recorded here. Arguably the best-known musical product of contemporary Ireland, they began as a band called The Hype in Mount Temple comprehensive school, on Malahide Road on Dublin's northside, back in the prehistory days of 1977. In March 1978, the four school pals teamed up to form U2. They started getting lots of attention in the media when they won a bands' competition in Limerick. During the rest of that year and through 1979, they performed a series of now legendary live concerts at such venues as the Dandelion Market, the Baggot Inn and Moran's Hotel, all in Dublin. These days, U2 are still regarded as one of the greatest musical acts of all time, yet they are incredibly loyal to their native city. Through them, they've helped engrave the image and the sound of Dublin on the hearts and minds of the world.

If you want to go 40 km (25 miles) out of town, try the Roundwood Inn in Co. Wicklow. It's off the N11, on the way to Glendalough. Garech de Brún, patron extraordinaire of Irish traditional music, closely connected with Claddagh Records, Dublin, lives nearby and he often drops in. Equally frequently, he will have star names from the music and entertainment world in tow, so if you want to rub shoulders with the likes of Van Morrison, this is the place.

Just as so much of the world-renowned Dublin music scene has its roots in the city's northside, à la U2, so too does much contemporary writing. The best-known of all contemporary Dublin writers, Roddy Doyle, born in 1958, is very much a northsider by birth, breeding and inclination, and in many ways the northside culture is the star of his works. He was educated at a national school in Raheny, at St Fintan's Christian Brothers school in Sutton (also on the northside) and then at the southside University College, Dublin. After he graduated, he taught for years at Greendale Community School in Kilbarrack, which is "Barrytown" in his fiction.

Entrance to the Gaiety Theatre, South King Street, Dublin

His first novel, *The Commitments*, published in 1989, showed an intimate knowledge of working-class Dublin. The 1990 book *The Snapper* was also set in this milieu, while the 1991 *The Van* tells of a mobile chipper in a poor, marginalised working-class suburb. Subsequent works, such as *Paddy Clarke Ha Ha Ha*, remain in the same setting. When his *Family* was done as a TV series, the actual filming took place in Ballymun, much to the annoyance of some local residents, who felt that the place was being unfairly stigmatised. A much more recent book has gone back to historical roots, *A Star called Henry* (1999); it's set in the first two decades of the 20th century and covers the Easter Rising period.

Another northside writer who is unashamedly proud of his roots is Dermot Bolger, poet, novelist, dramatist and publisher, who was born in another Dublin northside working-class suburb, Finglas. He was educated locally, at St Canice's and Beneavin College, before getting his first job, as a factory hand, in 1978–79. He went on to work as a library assistant from then until 1984. He has created a huge opus of work, much of it centred on, and inspired by, his origins in Finglas. His first novel, *Night Shift* (1985), was based on his time as a factory worker.

A slightly posher part of the northside is the milieu for another noted contemporary writer of popular and populist fiction, Patricia Scanlan. She was born in Glasnevin in 1956, educated at the Dominican convent in Eccles Street and worked at the community information centre in Ballymun before changing from librarian to writer. Her first novel, *City Girl*, published in 1990, was set in a luxury apartment block in Glasnevin, close to the pyramid-shaped Met Office.

If you'd like more information on the work and backgrounds of contemporary writers from Dublin and elsewhere in Ireland, contact: **Irish Writers Centre**, *19 Parnell Square, Dublin 1; tel (01) 872 1302; fax (01) 872 6282; website www.writerscentre.ie.*

Recommended Reading

All published by Appletree Press:

Ireland: The Complete Guide (new edition) by Hugh Oram
Ireland: A Traveller's Handbook
Dublin: The Complete Guide by Hugh Oram
North Ulster Walks by James Hamill
Walking the Ulster Way by Alan Warner
Walking Ireland's Mountains by David Herman
Bed and Breakfast Ireland by Elsie Dillard and Susan Causin
A Little History of Ireland by Martin Wallace
A Short History of Ireland by Martin Wallace
Irish Phrase Book by Paul Dorris
Pocket Irish Dictionary by Seosamh Watson
Complete Guide to Celtic Mythology by Bob Curran
Famous Irish Writers by Martin Wallace
Tracing Your Irish Roots by Christine Kinealy
Irish Family Names by Ida Grehan
The Book of Irish Names by Ronan Coghlan, Ida Grehan and
      P.W. Joyce
A Dictionary of Irish Place Names by Adrian Room
Ireland's Inland Waterways by Ruth Delany
The Complete Guide to The Quiet Man by Des MacHale
The Quiet Man and Other Stories by Maurice Walsh
The Coast of West Cork by Peter Somerville Large
The Irish Country Kitchen by Mary Kinsella
Traditional Irish Recipes by John Murphy
The Little Irish Cookbook by John Murphy
Off the Beaten Track: Irish Railway Walks by Kevin Cronin
Irish Battles: A Military History of Ireland by G.A. Hayes-
      McCoy
Irish Gardens by Terence Reeves-Smyth

The Custom House, Dublin

INDEX OF PLACES

Acknowledgements

The publisher wishes to thank the following for permission to publish their material:

Photographs
© Anthony Cassidy: pp 35, 38, 39, 166–7
Cork Kerry Tourism: p 115
© Dúchas, The Heritage Service: pp 15, 18, 19, 22, 27, 30 (top and bottom), 34, 42, 50, 51, 66, 79, 82, 83, 86, 122, 135 (top and bottom), 138
The Giant's Causeway & Bushmills Railway: p 99 (top and bottom)
© Irish Stock Library: pp 6–7, 54, 55, 58, 59, 63, 74, 91, 106, 128, 159, 162, 163
Hugh Oram: pp 150 (Louis Mulcahy), 154–5 (Belleek Pottery/Inform Public Relations)
Stock Pix: front cover, p 3

Map
Maps in Minutes™ © RH Publications

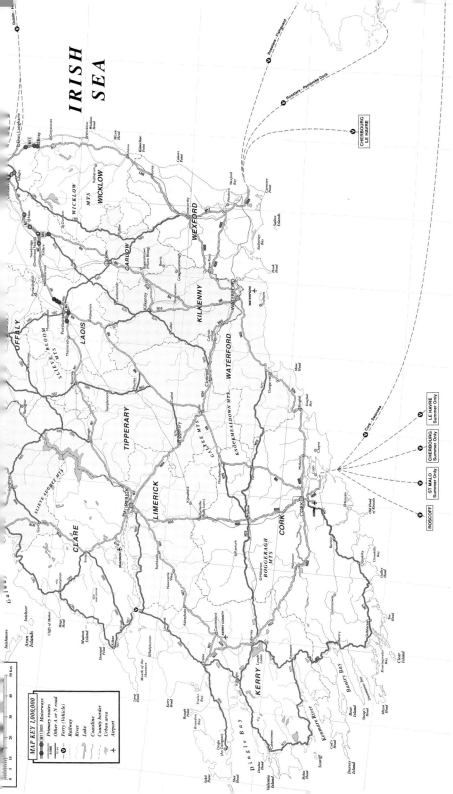